Hummingbirds
pages 4 - 5

Hometown
pages 6 - 7

Kansas Winter
pages 8 - 9

7 Sensational Quilts
with Scraps from Your Stash
or 'Jelly Roll' 2¹/₂" Strips

Grand Old Flag
pages 48 - 49

Baby Sampler
pages 47

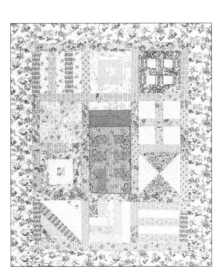

Cherry Blossoms
page 10

Something for Everyone
pages 50 - 51

'Fresh' Jelly Roll

Hummingbirds

pieced by Donna Perrotta
quilted by Julie Lawson

Prepare to fall in love again.

There is a common folk belief in Mexico that hummingbirds bring love and romance, making this quilt a perfect gift for an engaged couple, a wedding, or an anniversary celebration.

instructions on pages 17 - 20

'Glace' Jelly Roll

Hometown

pieced by Lanelle Herron
quilted by Susan Corbett

Step back into a simpler time with a friendly neighborhood of house blocks.

Set in easy-to-assemble columns, this quilt is quick to make and perfect for a housewarming gift or a thank you for your neighbor.

instructions on pages 21 - 23

'Kansas Winter'
Jelly Roll

Kansas Winter

pieced by Donna Arends Hansen
quilted by Sue Needle

Ward off Old Man Winter's chill with warm earth tones.

This quilt is perfect for snuggling with the kids in the family room or curling up beside the fire with your favorite book.

instructions on pages 24 - 25

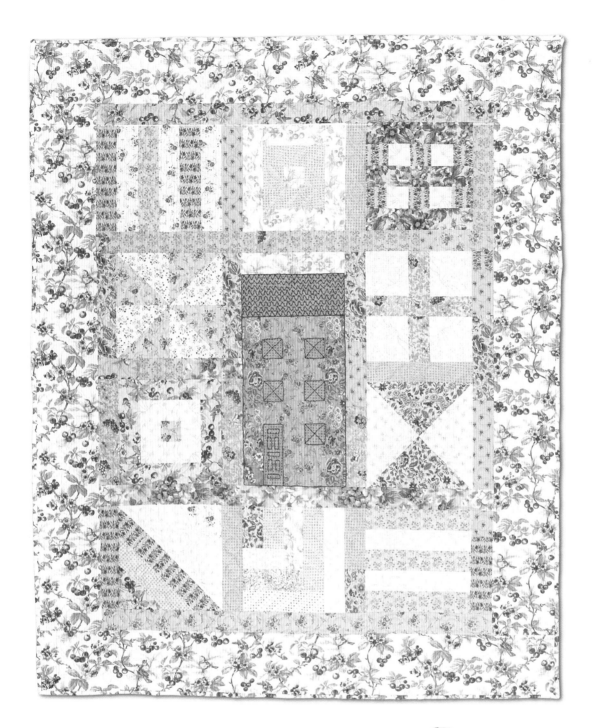

Cherry Blossoms

pieced by Kayleen Allen
quilted by Julie Lawson

Whispering soft promises of spring, these gentle colors will soothe your soul at the end of a long day.

This easy, breezy color palette coordinates beautifully with any home decor.

instructions on pages 11 -16

'Nostalgia'
Jelly Roll

Cherry Blossoms

photo is on page 10

SIZE: 50" x 62"

YARDAGE:
We used a *Moda* "Nostalgia" by April Cornell
  'Jelly Roll' collection of $2\frac{1}{2}$" fabric strips
  - we purchased 1 'Jelly Roll'

8 strips	OR	$\frac{5}{8}$ yard Color A - Ivory
8 strips	OR	$\frac{5}{8}$ yard Color B - Blue
9 strips	OR	$\frac{3}{4}$ yard Color C - Green
1 strip	OR	$\frac{1}{8}$ yard Color D - Red
2 strips	OR	$\frac{1}{6}$ yard Color E - Light Brown
Border & Binding		Purchase $1\frac{1}{2}$ yards Ivory print
Backing		Purchase $2\frac{7}{8}$ yards
Batting		Purchase 58" x 70"

Sewing machine, needle, thread

PREPARATION FOR STRIPS:
  Cut all strips $2\frac{1}{2}$" by the width of fabric (usually 42" - 44").
  Label the stacks or pieces as you cut.

SEW BLOCKS:
  Refer to the Cutting Chart and Assembly instructions for each
    block.
  Label the pieces as you cut.

GREEN SASHINGS:
  Cut 16 Vertical Sashes $2\frac{1}{2}$" x $10\frac{1}{2}$".
  Cut 2 Horizontal Sashes $2\frac{1}{2}$" x $14\frac{1}{2}$".
  Cut 4 Horizontal Sashes $2\frac{1}{2}$" x $38\frac{1}{2}$".

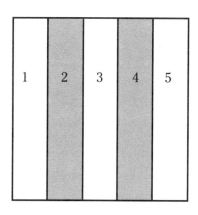

Vertical Stripe Block 2

Vertical Stripe · Block 2

CUTTING CHART

Quantity	Length	Position
Accent Color A - Ivory		
3	$10\frac{1}{2}$"	#1, 3, 5
Color B - Blue		
2	$10\frac{1}{2}$"	#2, 4

VERTICAL STRIPE BLOCK 2 ASSEMBLY:
Refer to the Block 1 diagram.
  Sew #1-2-3-4-5. Press.

House · Block 1

CUTTING CHART

Quantity	Length	Position
Color A - Ivory		
1	$10\frac{1}{2}$"	#18
Color E - Light Brown		
2	$16\frac{1}{2}$"	#14, 15
1	$10\frac{1}{2}$"	#8
2	$6\frac{1}{2}$"	#9, 13
1	$4\frac{1}{2}$"	#7
3	$2\frac{1}{2}$"	#2, 5, 11
Color D - Red		
2	$10\frac{1}{2}$"	#16, 17
1	$6\frac{1}{2}$"	#3
5	$2\frac{1}{2}$"	#1, 4, 6, 10, 12

HOUSE BLOCK 1 ASSEMBLY:
Refer to the Block 1 diagram.
  Sew #1-2-3. Press.
  Sew #4-5-6-7. Press.
  Sew #8 between #1-2-3 and #4-5-6-7. Press.
  Sew #9 to the top of the piece. Press.
  Sew #10-11-12. Press.
  Sew #10-11-12 & 13 to the top of the piece. Press.
  Sew #14 & #15 to the left and right sides of the piece. Press.
  Sew #16, 17 & 18 to the top of the piece. Press.

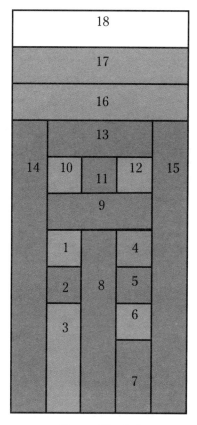

House Block 1

Courthouse Steps · Block 3

CUTTING CHART

Quantity	Length	Position
Color A - Ivory		
2	$10\frac{1}{2}$"	#8, 9
2	$6\frac{1}{2}$"	#6, 7
1	$2\frac{1}{2}$"	#2
Color B - Blue		
2	$6\frac{1}{2}$"	#4, 5
2	$2\frac{1}{2}$"	#1, 3

COURTHOUSE STEPS BLOCK 3 ASSEMBLY:
Refer to the Block 2 diagram.
    Sew #1-2-3. Press.
    Sew #4 & 5 to the top and bottom of the piece. Press.
    Sew #6 & 7 to the left and right sides of the piece. Press.
    Sew #8 & 9 to the top and bottom of the piece. Press.

Courthouse Steps Block 3

Cross · Block 4

CUTTING CHART

Quantity	Length	Position
Color A - Ivory		
2	5"	Unit 1
Color B - Blue		
3	$10\frac{1}{2}$"	#2, 3, 4
3	5"	Unit 1

CROSS BLOCK 4 ASSEMBLY:
Refer to the Block 3 diagram.
Unit 1: Sew 5" Unit 1 strips together
    Color B - Color A - Color B - Color A - Color B to
      make a piece 5" x $10\frac{1}{2}$". Press.
    Cut the piece into 2 sections $2\frac{1}{2}$" x $10\frac{1}{2}$". Press.
    Label each section Unit 1.
Assembly: Sew #2 - Unit 1 - #3 - Unit 1 - #4. Press.

Cross Block 4

Plus Sign · Block 6

CUTTING CHART

Quantity	Length	Position
Color A - Ivory		
4	9"	Unit 1
Color B - Blue		
1	9"	Unit 1
1	$10\frac{1}{2}$"	#2

PLUS SIGN BLOCK 6 ASSEMBLY:
Refer to the Block 6 diagram. .
Unit 1: Sew the 9" pieces together A-A-B-A-A to make a piece 9" x $10\frac{1}{2}$". Press.
    Cut the piece into 2 sections $4\frac{1}{2}$" x $10\frac{1}{2}$". Label each section Unit 1.
Assembly: Sew Unit 1 - #2 - Unit 1. Press.

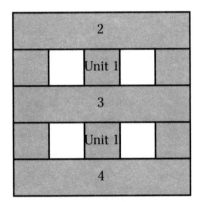

Plus Sign Block 6

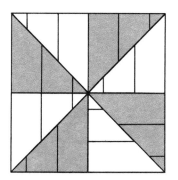

Pinwheel
Block 5

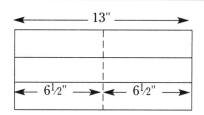

Pinwheel Block 5

CUTTING CHART

Quantity	Length	Position
Color A - Ivory		
3	13"	Half-Square Triangles
Color B - Blue		
3	13"	Half-Square Triangles

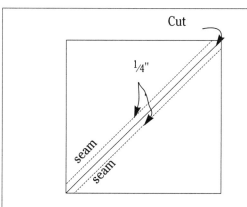

Half-Square Triangle
1. Place 2 squares right sides together.
2. Draw a diagonal line from corner to corner.
3. Sew a scant $1/4$" seam on each side of the line.
4. Cut squares apart on the diagonal line.
5. Open the 2 new squares with 2 colors.
6. Press. Trim off dog-ears.
7. Center and trim to size.

PREPARATION FOR PINWHEEL BLOCK 5
Sew 3 Color A strips together to make a piece $6^{1}/_{2}$" x 13".
Cut the piece in 2 squares $6^{1}/_{2}$" x $6^{1}/_{2}$".
Repeat for the Color B strips.

Each pair of A/B squares makes 2 Half-Square Triangle blocks.

HALF-SQUARE TRIANGLES:
Refer to Half-Square Triangle instructions.
Pair up a $6^{1}/_{2}$" Color A and a $6^{1}/_{2}$" Color B square with right sides together.
Draw a line from corner to corner on the diagonal.
Sew a scant $1/4$" seam on each side of the diagonal line.
Cut apart on the diagonal line to make 2 squares. Press.
Make 4 Half-Square Triangles.

Center and trim each Half-Square Triangle to $5^{1}/_{2}$" x $5^{1}/_{2}$".

ASSEMBLE A PINWHEEL:
Arrange 4 half-square triangles in a Pinwheel.
TIP: It is not necessary to match the interior seams.
Sew 2 rows of 2 blocks. Press.
Sew the rows together. Press.

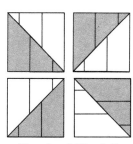

Pinwheel Block 5

Courthouse Steps · Block 7

CUTTING CHART

Quantity	Length	Position
Color A - Ivory		
2	$6^{1}/_{2}$"	#4, 5
2	$2^{1}/_{2}$"	#1, 3
Color B - Blue		
2	$10^{1}/_{2}$"	#8, 9
2	$6^{1}/_{2}$"	#6, 7
1	$2^{1}/_{2}$"	#2

COURTHOUSE STEPS BLOCK 7 ASSEMBLY:
Refer to the Block 7 diagram.
    Sew #1-2-3. Press.
    Sew #4 & 5 to the top and bottom of the piece. Press.
    Sew #6 & 7 to the left and right sides of the piece. Press.
    Sew #8 & 9 to the top and bottom of the piece. Press.

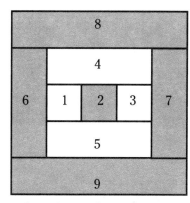

Courthouse Steps Block 7

Hourglass · Block 8

CUTTING CHART

Quantity	Length	Position
Color A - Ivory		
3	13"	Half-Square Triangles
Color B - Blue		
3	13"	Half-Square Triangles

HOURGLASS BLOCK 8 ASSEMBLY:
Half-Square Triangles: Follow the instructions given in Pinwheel Block 5.
Assembly: Arrange the half-square triangles following the Block 8 diagram.
  Sew 2 rows of 2 blocks each. Press.
  Sew the rows together. Press.

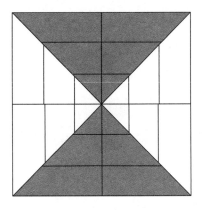

Hourglass Block 8

Strippy · Block 9

CUTTING CHART

Quantity	Length	Position
Color A - Ivory		
1	17"	#4
1	13"	#3
1	9"	#2
1	5"	#1
Color B - Blue		
1	17"	#5
1	13"	#6
1	9"	#7
1	5"	#8

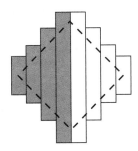

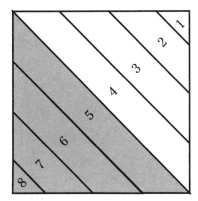

Strippy Block 9

STRIPPY BLOCK 9 ASSEMBLY:
Refer to the Block 9 diagram.
  Center and sew #1 on #2. Press.
  Center and sew #1-2 on #3. Press.
  Center and sew #1-2-3 on #4. Press.
  Repeat for #5,6,7,8. Sew 1-2-3-4 to 5-6-7-8. Press.
  Cut a $10\frac{1}{2}$" square on point.

Log Cabin · Block 10

CUTTING CHART

Quantity	Length	Position
Color A - Ivory		
1	$10\frac{1}{2}$"	#8
1	$8\frac{1}{2}$"	#7
1	$6\frac{1}{2}$"	#4
1	$4\frac{1}{2}$"	#3
Color B - Blue		
1	$8\frac{1}{2}$"	#6
1	$6\frac{1}{2}$"	#5
2	$4\frac{1}{2}$"	#1, 2

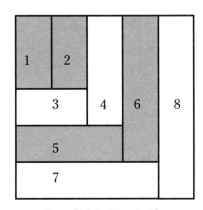

Log Cabin Block 10

LOG CABIN BLOCK 10 ASSEMBLY:
Refer to the Block 10 diagram.
  Sew #1-2. Press.
  Sew #3 to the bottom of the piece. Press.
  Sew #4 to the right side of the piece. Press.
  Sew #5 to the bottom of the piece. Press.
  Sew #6 to the right side of the piece. Press.
  Sew #7 to the bottom of the piece. Press.
  Sew #8 to the right side of the piece. Press.

Horizontal Stripe · Block 11

CUTTING CHART

Quantity	Length	Position
Color A - Ivory		
2	$10\frac{1}{2}$"	#2, 4
Color B - Blue		
3	$10\frac{1}{2}$"	#1, 3, 5

VERTICAL STRIPE BLOCK 11 ASSEMBLY:
Refer to the Block 11 diagram.
    Sew #1-2-3-4-5. Press.

Horizontal Stripe Block 11

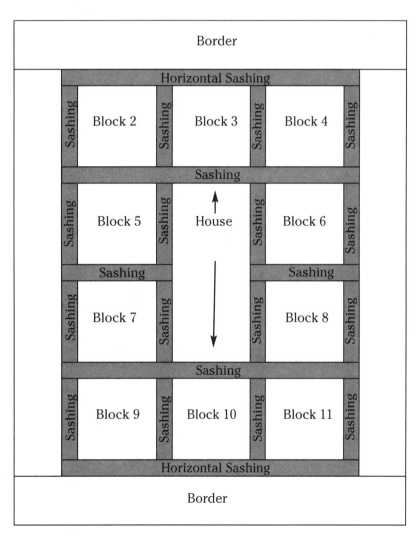

ASSEMBLY:
Refer to the Quilt Assembly diagram.
Arrange all blocks and sashes on a work surface.

Top Section:
    Use $10\frac{1}{2}$" vertical sashes between the blocks.
    Sew Sash - Block 2 - Sash - Block 3 - Sash -
        Block 4 - Sash. Press.
    Sew a $38\frac{1}{2}$" horizontal sash to the top and
        bottom of the piece.
        Press.

Center Section:
    Sew a $10\frac{1}{2}$" vertical sash to the left and right
        sides of Blocks 5, 6, 7, and 8. Press.
    Sew Blocks 5 & 7 together with a $14\frac{1}{2}$"
        horizontal sash between the blocks.
        Press.
    Repeat for Blocks 6 and 8.
    Sew #5-7 to the left side of House Block 1.
        Press.
    Sew #6-8 to the right sides of House Block 1.
        Press.

Bottom Section:
    Use $10\frac{1}{2}$" vertical sashes between the blocks.
    Sew Sash - Block 9 - Sash - Block 10 - Sash -
        Block 11 - Sash. Press.
    Sew a $38\frac{1}{2}$" horizontal sash to the top and
        bottom of the piece.
        Press.

Assembly:
    Sew the sections together. Press.

Cherry Blossoms
Assembly Diagram

Cherry Blossoms
Finished Diagram

BORDER:

Cut Ivory strips $6\frac{1}{2}$" wide parallel to the selvage to
    eliminate piecing.
    Cut 2 strips $6\frac{1}{2}$" x $50\frac{1}{2}$" for sides.
    Cut 2 strips $6\frac{1}{2}$" x $50\frac{1}{2}$" for top and bottom.
    Sew side borders to the quilt. Press.
    Sew top and bottom borders to the quilt. Press.

OPTIONAL EMBROIDERY:

Embroidery - pattern is below:
    Use Brown thread - Pearl Cotton or 6 ply floss
      and a #22 or #24 Chenille needle.
    Outline the House, Roof, Door and Windows
      with a Backstitch.
    Stitch an "X" in each window with a Backstitch.
    Stitch frame shapes on the door with a Backstitch.
    Stitch shingles on the roof witha Fly Stitch.

FINISHING:

Quilting: See Basic Instructions.
Binding: Cut strips $2\frac{1}{2}$" wide.
          Sew together end to end to equal 234".
          See Binding Instructions.

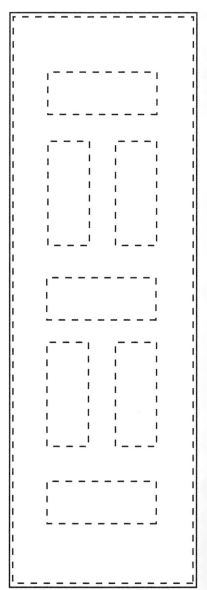

Cherry Blossom Door
Embroidery

Back Stitch

Come up at A, go
down at B. Come
back up at C.
Repeat.

Fly Stitch

Come up at A. Go down at B (right next to A) to
form a loop. Come back up at C with the needle
tip over the thread. Go down at D to make a small
anchor stitch over the top of the loop.

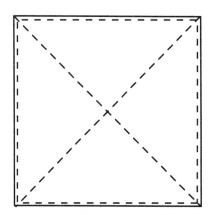

Cherry Blossom Window
Embroidery

Hummingbirds

photos are on pages 4 - 5

SIZE: 54" x 72"

YARDAGE:
We used a *Moda* "Fresh" by Deb Strain
'Jelly Roll' collection of $2\frac{1}{2}$" fabric strips
- we purchased 1 'Jelly Roll'
8 strips   OR $\frac{5}{8}$ yard Color B - Turquiose
7 strips   OR $\frac{1}{2}$ yard Color C - Green
5 strips   OR $\frac{3}{8}$ yard Color D - Orange/Red
5 strips   OR $\frac{3}{8}$ yard Color E - Yellow
3 strips   OR $\frac{1}{4}$ yard Color F - Orange
2 strips   OR $\frac{1}{6}$ yard Color G - Red
4 strips   OR $\frac{1}{3}$ yard Color H - White print
Accent Fabric A Purchase $\frac{3}{4}$ yards White print
Border #1 & Applique   Purchase $\frac{2}{3}$ yard Turquoise
Border #2 & Binding   Purchase $1\frac{7}{8}$ yards
Backing   Purchase $3\frac{1}{3}$ yards
Batting   Purchase 62" x 80"
4 Black $\frac{1}{8}$" buttons
Sewing machine, needle, thread

PREPARATION FOR APPLIQUE:
Fabric or Scraps for 1 Hummingbird Applique:
   Background Blocks -
   From Accent Color A - White print,
      cut 4 squares $12\frac{1}{2}$" x $12\frac{1}{2}$".

   Hummingbirds
   Pull out 1 strip of each for hummingbird applique.
      1 strip of Red - throat   **Note:** Wings & body
      1 strip of Orange - beak   top are cut from
      1 strip of Turquoise - belly   Turquoise yardage.

   Note:
   This leaves 27 strips to make 54 Courthouse Steps blocks.

PREPARATION FOR STRIPS:
   Cut all strips $2\frac{1}{2}$" by the width of fabric (usually 42" - 44").
   Label the stacks or pieces as you cut.

FABRIC FOR INDIVIDUAL BLOCKS:
Fabric or Scraps for 1 Courthouse Steps Block:
   You will need 4 strips of White print and
      27 strips of colors B,C,D,E,F, or G

   Color H - White print $2\frac{1}{2}$" x $2\frac{1}{2}$"
   Color strip (B,C,D,E,F, or G) $2\frac{1}{2}$" x 18" OR $\frac{1}{2}$ strip

CUTTING CHART
For 2 Courthouse Steps Blocks:

Quantity	Length	Position	Total
Color H - use 3 strips of White print			
1	5"	Center unit	Total - 27
Color strips - use 27 strips of colors B,C,D,E,F, or G			
4	$6\frac{1}{2}$"	#1, 2	Total - 108
2	5"	Center unit	Total - 54

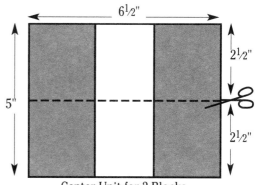

Center Unit for 2 Blocks

SEW BLOCKS:
   Sew 2 blocks at one time.
   Note: Each color strip will be used to make 2 blocks.

Assemble the Center Unit:
   Sew 2 Color and 1 White 5" strips together
      C-W-C to make a piece 5" x $6\frac{1}{2}$". Press.
   Cut 2 pieces $2\frac{1}{2}$" x $6\frac{1}{2}$".

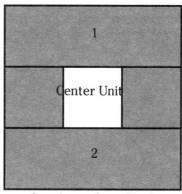

Courthouse Steps Block

Assemble the Block:
Note: Make 2 blocks from each color strip.

Sew a $6\frac{1}{2}$" strip to the top and bottom of a Center Unit. Press.
The block will measure $6\frac{1}{2}$" x $6\frac{1}{2}$".

HUMMINGBIRD APPLIQUE BLOCKS:
   Refer to the Applique instructions.
   Cut out pieces using the patterns.
   Applique as desired.

   The block will measure $12\frac{1}{2}$" x $12\frac{1}{2}$".
   Make 4 blocks.

ASSEMBLY:

Refer to the Quilt Assembly diagram.
Arrange all blocks on a work surface or table.

Rows 1, 3, 5, 6:

Sew 7 blocks together. Press.

Rows
2 & 4

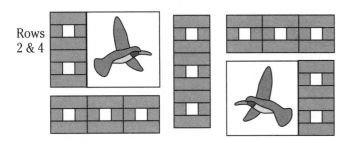

Rows 2 & 4:

Sew 2 blocks together vertically. Press.
Sew to left side of right facing bird. Press.
Sew 3 blocks together horizontally. Press.
Sew to bottom of the piece. Press.
Sew 3 blocks together vertically. Press.
Sew to right side of the piece. Press.
Sew 2 blocks together vertically. Press.
Sew to right side of left facing bird. Press.
Sew 3 blocks together horizontally. Press.
Sew to the top of the piece. Press.
Sew left section to right section. Press.
Make 2.

Sew rows together. Press.

BORDERS:
Border #1:
Sew Turquoise strips together end to end.

Cut 2 strips 2½" x 60½" for sides.
Cut 2 strips 2½" x 46½" for top and bottom.

Sew side borders to the quilt. Press.
Sew top and bottom borders to the quilt. Press.

Border #2:
Cut strips 4½" wide parallel to the selvage to eliminate piecing.

Cut 2 strips 4½" x 64½" for sides.
Cut 2 strips 4½" x 54½" for top and bottom.

Sew side borders to the quilt. Press.
Sew top and bottom borders to the quilt. Press.

FINISHING:
Quilting:
See Basic Instructions.

Binding:
Cut strips 2½" wide.
Sew together end to end to equal 262".
See Binding Instructions.

Sew Black buttons for hummingbird eyes.

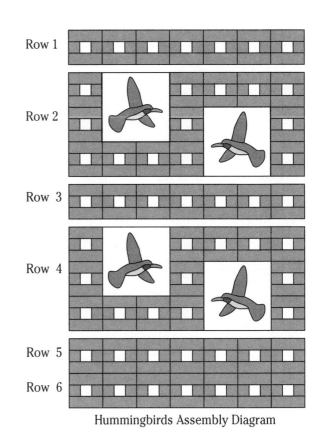

Row 1
Row 2
Row 3
Row 4
Row 5
Row 6

Hummingbirds Assembly Diagram

Hummingbirds Finished Assembly Diagram

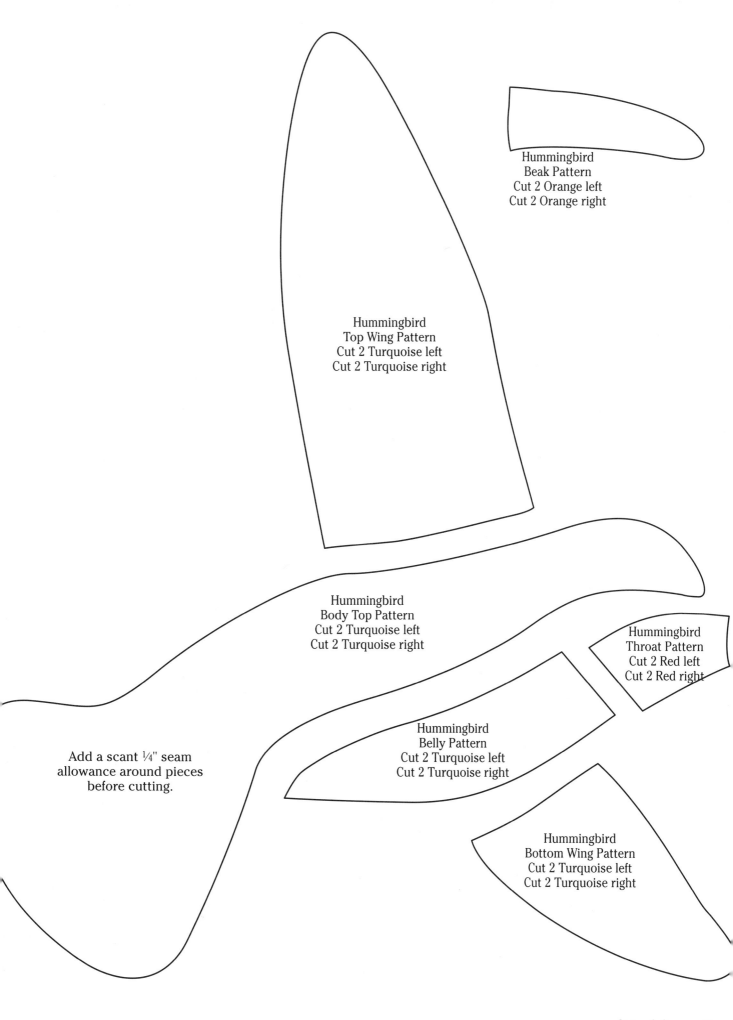

Hummingbird
Beak Pattern
Cut 2 Orange left
Cut 2 Orange right

Hummingbird
Top Wing Pattern
Cut 2 Turquoise left
Cut 2 Turquoise right

Hummingbird
Body Top Pattern
Cut 2 Turquoise left
Cut 2 Turquoise right

Hummingbird
Throat Pattern
Cut 2 Red left
Cut 2 Red right

Hummingbird
Belly Pattern
Cut 2 Turquoise left
Cut 2 Turquoise right

Add a scant ¼" seam
allowance around pieces
before cutting.

Hummingbird
Bottom Wing Pattern
Cut 2 Turquoise left
Cut 2 Turquoise right

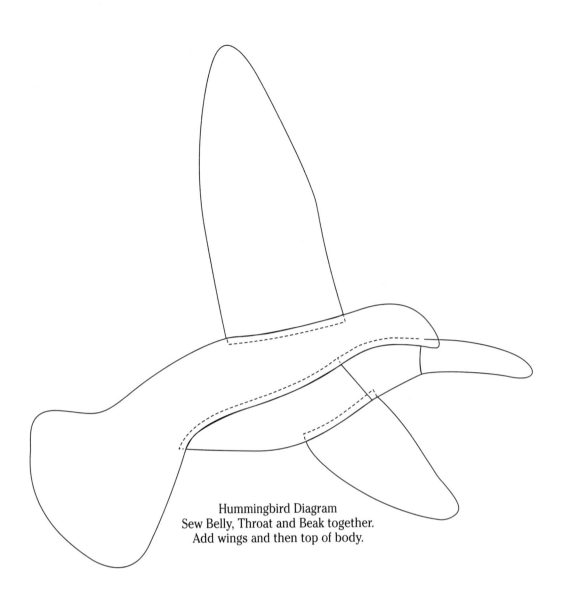

Hummingbird Diagram
Sew Belly, Throat and Beak together.
Add wings and then top of body.

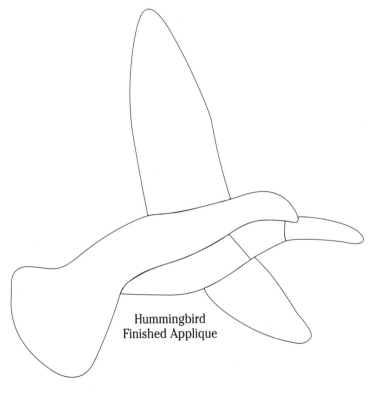

Hummingbird
Finished Applique

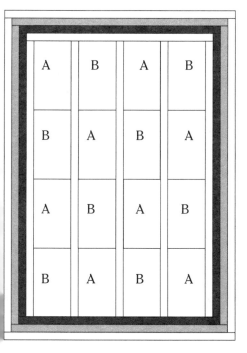

Hometown - Assembly Diagram

Hometown
Larger Quilt

no photo of the large quilt is available

SIZE: 62" x 86

YARDAGE:
We used a *Moda* "Glace" by 3 Sisters
    'Jelly Roll' collection of $2\frac{1}{2}$" fabric strips
    - we purchased 2 'Jelly Rolls'

18 strips	OR	$1\frac{1}{4}$ yard Color D - Green
16 strips	OR	$1\frac{1}{4}$ yard Color E - Brown
12 strips	OR	1 yard Color B - Red
12 strips	OR	1 yard Color C - Blue

Accent Fabric A	Purchase 2 yards Ivory
Binding	Use Ivory Accent Fabric
Backing	Purchase $6\frac{1}{2}$ yards
Batting	Purchase 70" x 96"

Sewing machine, needle, thread

BLOCKS:
Refer to the Block instructions to make 8 of Block A and
    8 of Block B.

SASHINGS:
    Cut 5 Ivory Vertical Sashing strips $2\frac{1}{2}$" x $72\frac{1}{2}$".
    Cut 1 Ivory Horizontal Sashing strip $2\frac{1}{2}$" x $50\frac{1}{2}$".

ASSEMBLY:
Refer to the Quilt Assembly diagram.
Arrange all blocks and sashings on a work surface.

Columns 1 & 3:
    Sew a House A - House B - House A - House B.
    Press.
Columns 2 & 4:
    Sew a House B - House A - House B - House A
    Press.
Assembly:
    Sew a Vertical Sash - Column 1- Vertical Sash
        - Column 2 - Vertical Sash - Column 3
         - Vertical Sash - Column 4 - Vertical Sash. Press.
    Sew a Horizontal Sash to the top and to the bottom
        of the quilt. Press.

BORDERS:
Border #1:
Sew 7 Brown strips together end to end.
    Cut 2 strips $2\frac{1}{2}$" x $74\frac{1}{2}$" for sides.
    Cut 2 strips $2\frac{1}{2}$" x $54\frac{1}{2}$" for top and bottom.
Border #2:
Sew 7 Green strips together end to end.
    Cut 2 strips $2\frac{1}{2}$" x $78\frac{1}{2}$" for sides.
    Cut 2 strips $2\frac{1}{2}$" x $58\frac{1}{2}$" for top and bottom.
Border #3:
Cut 7 Ivory strips and sew together end to end.
    Cut 2 strips $2\frac{1}{2}$" x $82\frac{1}{2}$" for sides.
    Cut 2 strips $2\frac{1}{2}$" x $62\frac{1}{2}$" for top and bottom.

FINISHING:
Sew quilt together then layer and attach the binding.

Hometown - Finished Diagram

Hometown

photos are on pages 6 - 7

SIZE: 50" x 68"

YARDAGE:
We used a *Moda* "Glace" by 3 Sisters
   'Jelly Roll' collection of $2\frac{1}{2}$" fabric strips
   - we purchased 1 'Jelly Roll'
9 strips	OR	$\frac{5}{8}$ yard Color D - Green
8 strips	OR	$\frac{5}{8}$ yard Color E - Brown
6 strips	OR	$\frac{1}{2}$ yard Color B - Red
6 strips	OR	$\frac{1}{2}$ yard Color C - Blue
6 strips	OR	$\frac{1}{2}$ yard Color F - Ivory - Border #3

Accent Fabric A	Purchase $1\frac{5}{8}$ yards Ivory
Binding	Use Ivory Accent Fabric
Backing	Purchase $3\frac{1}{8}$ yards
Batting	Purchase 58" x 76"

Sewing machine, needle, thread

FABRIC FOR INDIVIDUAL BLOCKS:
Fabric or Scraps for 1 of Tall House Block A:
1 strip	OR	$2\frac{1}{2}$" x $10\frac{1}{2}$" of Color A - Ivory
1 strip	OR	$2\frac{1}{2}$" x $42\frac{1}{2}$" of Color B - Red
1 strip	OR	$2\frac{1}{2}$" x 43" of Color C - Blue

Fabric or Scraps for 1 of Short House Block B:
1 strip	OR	$2\frac{1}{2}$" x $28\frac{1}{2}$" of Color E - Brown
1 strip	OR	$2\frac{1}{2}$" x $34\frac{1}{2}$" of Color D - Green
1 strip	OR	$2\frac{1}{2}$" x 35" of Color A - Ivory

PREPARATION FOR STRIPS:
Cut all strips $2\frac{1}{2}$" by the width of fabric (usually 42" - 44").
Label the stacks or pieces as you cut.

SEW BLOCKS:
Refer to the Cutting Chart and Assembly instructions for each block.
Label the pieces as you cut.

SASHINGS:
Cut 4 Ivory Vertical Sashing strips $2\frac{1}{2}$" x $54\frac{1}{2}$".
Cut 1 Ivory Horizontal Sashing strip $2\frac{1}{2}$" x $38\frac{1}{2}$".

ASSEMBLY:
Refer to the Quilt Assembly diagram.
Arrange all blocks and sashings on a work surface or table.
Columns 1 & 3:
Sew a Tall House A - Short House B - Tall House A. Press.
Column 2:
Sew a Short House B - Tall House A - Short House B. Press.
Assembly:
Sew a Vertical Sash - Column 1 - Vertical Sash - Column 2 - Vertical Sash - Column 3 - Vertical Sash. Press.
Sew a Horizontal Sash to the top of the quilt. Press.

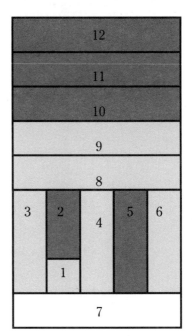

Tall House - Block A

For 1 of Tall House Block A:
Cut all strips $2\frac{1}{2}$" wide.

CUTTING CHART
Quantity	Length	Position
Accent Color A - Ivory		
1	$10\frac{1}{2}$"	#7
Color B - Red		
3	$10\frac{1}{2}$"	#10, 11, 12
1	$6\frac{1}{2}$"	#5
1	$4\frac{1}{2}$"	#2
Color C - Blue		
2	$10\frac{1}{2}$"	#8, 9
3	$6\frac{1}{2}$"	#3, 4, 6
1	$2\frac{1}{2}$"	#1

Tall House · Block A

ASSEMBLY:
Refer to the Block A diagram. Make 5.
   Sew #1-2. Press.
   Sew #3 on the left side of #1-2. Press.
   Sew #4, 5 & 6 to the right side of the piece. Press.
   Sew #7 to the bottom of the piece. Press.
   Sew #8, 9, 10, 11, & 12 to the top of the piece. Press.

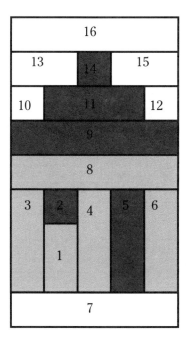

Short House - Block B

For 1 of Short House Block B:

Cut all strips $2\frac{1}{2}$" wide.

CUTTING CHART

Quantity	Length	Position
Accent Color A - Ivory		
2	$10\frac{1}{2}$"	#7, 16
2	$4\frac{1}{2}$"	#13, 15
2	$2\frac{1}{2}$"	#10, 12
Color E - Brown		
1	$10\frac{1}{2}$"	#9
2	$6\frac{1}{2}$"	#5, 11
2	$2\frac{1}{2}$"	#2, 14
Color D - Green		
1	$10\frac{1}{2}$"	#8
3	$6\frac{1}{2}$"	#3, 4, 6
1	$4\frac{1}{2}$"	#1

Short House · Block B

ASSEMBLY:

Refer to the Block A diagram. Make 4.

Sew #1-2. Press.

Sew #3 on the left side of #1-2. Press.

Sew #4, 5 & 6 to the right side of the piece. Press.

Sew #7 to the bottom of the piece. Press.

Sew #8 & 9 to the top of the house. Press.

Sew #10-11-12. Press. Sew to the top of the house. Press.

Sew #13-14-15. Press. Sew to the top of the house. Press.

Sew #16 to the top of the house. Press.

BORDERS:

Border #1:

Sew 5 Brown strips together end to end.

Cut 2 strips $2\frac{1}{2}$" x $56\frac{1}{2}$" for sides.

Cut 2 strips $2\frac{1}{2}$" x $42\frac{1}{2}$" for top and bottom.

Sew side borders to the quilt. Press.

Sew top and bottom borders to the quilt. Press.

Border #2:

Sew 6 Green strips together end to end.

Cut 2 strips $2\frac{1}{2}$" x $60\frac{1}{2}$" for sides.

Cut 2 strips $2\frac{1}{2}$" x $46\frac{1}{2}$" for top and bottom.

Sew side borders to the quilt. Press.

Sew top and bottom borders to the quilt. Press.

Border #3:

Cut 6 Ivory strips and sew together end to end.

Cut 2 strips $2\frac{1}{2}$" x $64\frac{1}{2}$" for sides.

Cut 2 strips $2\frac{1}{2}$" x $50\frac{1}{2}$" for top and bottom.

Sew side borders to the quilt. Press.

Sew top and bottom borders to the quilt. Press.

FINISHING:

Quilting: See Basic Instructions.

Binding: Cut strips $2\frac{1}{2}$" wide.

Sew together end to end to equal 246".

Note: We used 6 leftover Light strips.

See Binding Instructions.

Hometown Quilt - Finished Assembly Diagram

Kansas Winter

photos are on pages 8 - 9

SIZE: 60" x 76"

YARDAGE:
We used a *Moda* "Basics" Black
   'Jelly Roll' collection of $2\frac{1}{2}$" fabric strips
   - we purchased 1 'Jelly Roll'
   23 strips   OR $1\frac{5}{8}$ yards Fabric A - Black
We used a *Moda* "Kansas Winter" by Kansas Troubles
   'Jelly Roll' collection of $2\frac{1}{2}$" fabric strips
   - we purchased 1 'Jelly Roll'
   3 strips   OR $\frac{1}{4}$ yard Color D - Red
   7 strips   OR $\frac{1}{2}$ yard Color B - Ivory
   14 strips   OR   1 yard Color C - Assorted Green,
                               Gold, Tan, Black print
Border #2 & Binding   Purchase 2 yards Black print
Backing   Purchase $3\frac{5}{8}$ yards
Batting   Purchase 68" x 84"
Sewing machine, needle, thread

FABRIC FOR INDIVIDUAL BLOCKS:

Fabric or Scraps for 1 Log Cabin Block:
   2 strips   OR $2\frac{1}{2}$" x 57" of Accent Color A - Black
   1 strip   OR $2\frac{1}{2}$" x 23" of Color B - Ivory
   2 strips   OR $2\frac{1}{2}$" x $46\frac{1}{2}$" of Color C (assorted colors)
   1 strip   OR $2\frac{1}{2}$" x 9" of Color D - Red

PREPARATION FOR STRIPS:
Cut all strips $2\frac{1}{2}$" by the width of fabric (usually 42" - 44").
Label the stacks or pieces as you cut.

CUTTING CHART
For 12 Log Cabin Blocks:

Quantity	Length	Position
Color A - Black		
1	$40\frac{1}{2}$"	Center unit
1	$13\frac{1}{2}$"	Center unit
12	$14\frac{1}{2}$"	#9
12	$12\frac{1}{2}$"	#8
12	$10\frac{1}{2}$"	#5
12	$8\frac{1}{2}$"	#4
12	$6\frac{1}{2}$"	#1
Color D - Red		
2	$40\frac{1}{2}$"	Center unit
2	$13\frac{1}{2}$"	Center unit
Color B - Ivory		
12	$12\frac{1}{2}$"	#7
12	$10\frac{1}{2}$"	#6
Color C - Assorted & Leftover colors		
(Green, Gold, Tan, Black print, Red)		
12	$16\frac{1}{2}$"	#11
12	$14\frac{1}{2}$"	#10
12	$8\frac{1}{2}$"	#3
12	$6\frac{1}{2}$"	#2

SEW BLOCKS:
Refer to the Cutting Chart.
Label the pieces as you cut.

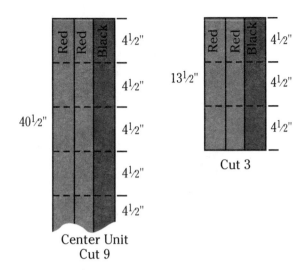

Center Unit
Cut 9

Cut 3

LOG CABIN BLOCK ASSEMBLY:
Center Unit:
   Sew 2 Red and 1 Black $40\frac{1}{2}$" strips together
   R-R-B to make a piece $6\frac{1}{2}$" x $40\frac{1}{2}$". Press.
   Sew 2 Red and 1 Black $13\frac{1}{2}$" strips together
   R-R-B to make a piece $6\frac{1}{2}$" x $13\frac{1}{2}$". Press.
   Cut a total of 12 pieces $4\frac{1}{2}$" x $6\frac{1}{2}$".

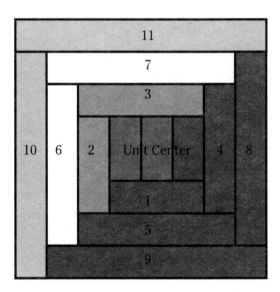

Add Log Cabin Rows to the Block:
   Sew #1 to the bottom of the Center Unit. Press.
   Sew #2 to the left side. Press.
   Sew #3 to the top and #4 to the right hand side. Press.

   Continue sewing strips in order. Press.
   Each block will measure $16\frac{1}{2}$" x $16\frac{1}{2}$".

   Make 12 blocks.

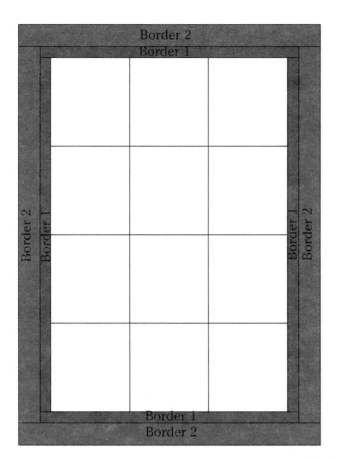

ASSEMBLE THE QUILT:
  Refer to the Quilt Assembly diagram.
  Arrange all blocks on a work surface or table.

  Note: Refer to the diagonal and color position of each block.
  Sew 3 blocks together side by side.
    Repeat to make 4 rows. Press.
  Sew all 4 rows together. Press.

BORDERS:
Border #1:
Sew Black strips together end to end.
  Cut 2 strips $2\frac{1}{2}$" x $64\frac{1}{2}$" for sides.
  Cut 2 strips $2\frac{1}{2}$" x $52\frac{1}{2}$" for top and bottom.
  Sew side borders to the quilt. Press.
  Sew top and bottom borders to the quilt. Press.

Border #2:
Cut strips $4\frac{1}{2}$" wide parallel to the selvage to eliminate piecing.
  Cut 2 strips $4\frac{1}{2}$" x $68\frac{1}{2}$" for sides.
  Cut 2 strips $4\frac{1}{2}$" x $60\frac{1}{2}$" for top and bottom.
  Sew side borders to the quilt. Press.
  Sew top and bottom borders to the quilt. Press.

FINISHING:
Quilting:
  See Basic Instructions.

Binding:
  Cut strips $2\frac{1}{2}$" wide.
  Sew together end to end to equal 282".
  See Binding Instructions.

Kansas Winter
Assembly Diagram

The Best Things About 'Jelly Rolls'

I love to quilt, but it is often difficult to find time to cut and piece a quilt top. When I saw collections of 2½" pre-cut fabric strips, I knew they were the answer.

No more spending hours choosing and cutting fabrics. Now I can begin sewing right away. Beautiful colors are available in every set. So whether I like jewel colors, heritage patterns, soft pastels or earthy tones... there is an assortment for me.

Now my goals... a handmade cover for every bed, an heirloom quilt for each new baby and a pieced quilt for each of my children... are within reach. With 'Jelly Rolls' it is possible to complete a quilt top in a weekend.

After I piece all the blocks together, I use leftover strips for the borders and binding. Nothing really goes to waste and, if needed, I can purchase a bit of extra fabric for an extra punch of color or an additional yard for the border.

TIP: Quantities are given in strips and yardage so you know what you need and can start right away.

Tips for Working with Strips

Guide for Yardage:

2½" Strips - Each ¼ yard or a 'Fat Quarter' equals 3 strips - A pre-cut 'Jelly Roll' strip is 2½" x 44"

Pre-cut strips are cut on the crosswise grain and are prone to stretching. These tips will help reduce stretching and make your quilt lay flat for quilting.

1. If you are cutting yardage, cut on the grain. Cut fat quarters on grain, parallel to the 18" side.

2. When sewing crosswise grain strips together, take care not to stretch the strips. If you detect any puckering as you go, rip out the seam and sew it again.

3. Press, Do Not Iron. Carefully open fabric, with the seam to one side, press without moving the iron. A back-and-forth ironing motion stretches the fabric.

4. Reduce the wiggle in your borders with this technique from garment making. First, accurately cut your borders to the exact measure of the quilt top. Then, before sewing the border to the quilt, run a double row of stay stitches along the outside edge to maintain the original shape and prevent stretching. Pin the border to the quilt, taking care not to stretch the quilt top to make it fit. Pinning reduces slipping and stretching.

Rotary Cutting

Rotary Cutter: Friend or Foe

A rotary cutter is wonderful and useful. When not used correctly, the sharp blade can be a dangerous tool. Follow these safety tips:

1. Never cut toward you.

2. Use a sharp blade. Pressing harder on a dull blade can cause the blade to jump the ruler and injure your fingers.

3. Always disengage the blade before the cutter leaves your hand, even if you intend to pick it up immediately.

Rotary cutters have been caught when lifting fabric, have fallen onto the floor and have cut fingers.

Basic Sewing

You now have precisely cut strips that are exactly the correct width. You are well on your way to blocks that fit together perfectly. Accurate sewing is the next important step.

Matching Edges:

1. Carefully line up the edges of your strips. Many times, if the underside is off a little, your seam will be off by $\frac{1}{8}$". This does not sound like much until you have 8 seams in a block, each off by $\frac{1}{8}$". Now your finished block is a whole inch wrong!

2. Pin the pieces together to prevent them shifting.

Seam Allowance:

I cannot stress enough the importance of accurate $\frac{1}{4}$" seams. All the quilts in this book are measured for $\frac{1}{4}$" seams unless otherwise indicated.

Most sewing machine manufacturers offer a Quarter-inch foot. A Quarter-inch foot is the most worthwhile investment you can make in your quilting.

Pressing:

I want to talk about pressing even before we get to sewing because proper pressing can make the difference between a quilt that wins a ribbon at the quilt show and one that does not.

Press, do NOT iron. What does that mean? Many of us want to move the iron back and forth along the seam. This "ironing" stretches the strip out of shape and creates errors that accumulate as the quilt is constructed. Believe it or not, there is a correct way to press your seams, and here it is:

1. Do NOT use steam with your iron. If you need a little water, spritz it on.

2. Place your fabric flat on the ironing board without opening the seam. Set a hot iron on the seam and count to 3. Lift the iron and move to the next position along the seam. Repeat until the entire seam is pressed. This sets and sinks the threads into the fabric.

3. Now, carefully lift the top strip and fold it away from you so the seam is on one side. Usually the seam is pressed toward the darker fabric, but often the direction of the seam is determined by the piecing requirements.

4. Press the seam open with your fingers. Add a little water or spray starch if it wants to close again. Lift the iron and place it on the seam. Count to 3. Lift the iron again and continue until the seam is pressed. Do NOT use the tip of the iron to push the seam open. So many people do this and wonder later why their blocks are not fitting together.

5. Most critical of all: For accuracy every seam must be pressed before the next seam is sewn.

Working with 'Crosswise Grain' Strips:

Strips cut on the crosswise grain (from selvage to selvage) have problems similar to bias edges and are prone to stretching. To reduce stretching and make your quilt lay flat for quilting, keep these tips in mind.

1. Take care not to stretch the strips as you sew.

2. Adjust the sewing thread tension and the presser foot pressure if needed.

3. If you detect any puckering as you go, rip out the seam and sew it again. It is much easier to take out a seam now than to do it after the block is sewn.

Sewing Bias Edges:

Bias edges wiggle and stretch out of shape very easily. They are not recommended for beginners, but even a novice can accomplish bias edges if these techniques are employed.

1. Stabilize the bias edge with one of these methods:

a) Press with spray starch.

b) Press freezer paper or removable iron-on stabilizer to the back of the fabric.

c) Sew a double row of stay stitches along the bias edge and $\frac{1}{8}$" from the bias edge. This is a favorite technique of garment makers.

2. Pin, pin, pin! I know many of us dislike pinning, but when working with bias edges, pinning makes the difference between intersections that match and those that do not.

Building Better Borders:

Wiggly borders make a quilt very difficult to finish. However, wiggly borders can be avoided with these techniques.

1. Cut the borders on grain. That means cutting your strips parallel to the selvage edge.

2. Accurately cut your borders to the exact measure of the quilt.

3. If your borders are piece stripped from crosswise grain fabrics, press well with spray starch and sew a double row of stay stitches along the outside edge to maintain the original shape and prevent stretching.

4. Pin the border to the quilt, taking care not to stretch the quilt top to make it fit. Pinning reduces slipping and stretching.

Embroidery Use 24" lengths of doubled pearl cotton or 6-ply floss and a #22 or #24 Chenille needle (this needle has a large eye). Outline large elements.

Running Stitch Come up at A. Weave the needle through the fabric, making LONG stitches on the top and SHORT stitches on the bottom. Keep stitches even.

Applique Instructions

Basic Turned Edge

1. Trace pattern onto no-melt template plastic (or onto Wash-Away Tear-Away Stabilizer).

2. Cut out the fabric shape leaving a scant $1/4$" fabric border all around and clip the curves.

3. **Plastic Template Method -** Place plastic shape on the wrong side of the fabric. Spray edges with starch. Press a $1/4$" border over the edge of the template plastic with the tip of a hot iron. Press firmly.

4. **Stabilizer Method -** Place stabilizer shape on the wrong side of the fabric. Use a glue stick to press a $1/4$" border over the edge of the stabilizer securing it with the glue stick. Press firmly.

5. Remove the template, maintaining the folded edge on the back of the fabric.

6. Position the shape on the quilt and Blindstitch in place.

Basic Turned Edge by Hand

1. Cut out the shape leaving a $1/4$" fabric border all around.

2. Baste the shapes to the quilt, keeping the basting stitches away from the edge of the fabric.

3. Begin with all areas that are under other layers and work to the topmost layer.

4. For an area no more than 2" ahead of where you are working, trim to $1/8$" and clip the curves.

5. Using the needle, roll the edge under and sew tiny Blindstitches to secure.

Using Fusible Web for Iron-on Applique:

1. Trace pattern onto Steam a Seam 2 fusible web.

2. Press the patterns onto the wrong side of fabric.

3. Cut out patterns exactly on the drawn line.

4. Score web paper with a pin, then remove the paper.

5. Position the fabric, fusible side down, on the quilt. Press with a hot iron following the fusible web manufacturer's instructions.

6. Stitch around the edge by hand.

Optional: Stabilize the wrong side of the fabric with your favorite stabilizer.

Use a size 80 machine embroidery needle. Fill the bobbin with lightweight basting thread and thread machine with machine embroidery thread that complements the color being appliqued.

Set your machine for a Zigzag stitch and adjust the thread tension if needed. Use a scrap to experiment with different stitch widths and lengths until you find the one you like best.

Sew slowly.

Basic Layering Instructions

Marking Your Quilt:

If you choose to mark your quilt for hand or machine quilting, it is much easier to do so before layering. Press your quilt before you begin. Here are some handy tips regarding marking.

1. A disappearing pen may vanish before you finish.

2. Use a White pencil on dark fabrics.

3. If using a washable Blue pen, remember that pressing may make the pen permanent.

Pieced Backings:

1. Press the backing fabric before measuring.

2. If possible cut backing fabrics on grain, parallel to the selvage edges.

3. Piece 3 parts rather than 2 whenever possible, sewing 2 side borders to the center. This reduces stress on the pieced seam.

4. Backing and batting should extend at least 2" on each side of the quilt.

Creating a Quilt Sandwich:

1. Press the backing and top to remove all wrinkles.

2. Lay the backing wrong side up on the table.

3. Position the batting over the backing and smooth out all wrinkles.

4. Center the quilt top over the batting leaving a 2" border all around.

5. Pin the layers together with 2" safety pins positioned a handwidth apart. A grapefruit spoon makes inserting the pins easier. Leaving the pins open in the container speeds up the basting on the next quilt.

Basic Quilting Instructions

Hand Quilting:

Many quilters enjoy the serenity of hand quilting. Because the quilt is handled a great deal, it is important to securely baste the sandwich together. Place the quilt in a hoop and don't forget to hide your knots.

Machine Quilting:

All the quilts in this book were machine quilted. Some were quilted on a large, free-arm quilting machine and others were quilted on a sewing machine. If you have never machine quilted before, practice on some scraps first.

Straight Line Machine Quilting Tips:

1. Pin baste the layers securely.

2. Set up your sewing machine with a size 80 quilting needle and a walking foot.

3. Experimenting with the decorative stitches on your machine adds interest to your quilt. You do not have to quilt the entire piece with the same stitch. Variety is the spice of life, so have fun trying out stitches you have never used before as well as your favorite stand-bys.

Free Motion Machine Quilting Tips:

1. Pin baste the layers securely.

2. Set up your sewing machine with a spring needle, a quilting foot, and lower the feed dogs.

Basic Mitered Binding

A Perfect Finish:

The binding endures the most stress on a quilt and is usually the first thing to wear out. For this reason, we recommend using a double fold binding.

1. Trim the backing and batting even with the quilt edge.

2. If possible cut strips on the crosswise grain because a little bias in the binding is a Good thing. This is the only place in the quilt where bias is helpful, for it allows the binding to give as it is turned to the back and sewn in place.

3. Strips are usually cut 2½" wide, but check the instructions for your project before cutting.

4. Sew strips end to end to make a long strip sufficient to go all around the quilt plus 4"- 6".

5. With wrong sides together, fold the strip in half lengthwise. Press.

6. Stretch out your hand and place your little finger at the corner of the quilt top. Place the binding where your thumb touches the edge of the quilt. Aligning the edge of the quilt with the raw edges of the binding, pin the binding in place along the first side.

7. Leaving a 2" tail for later use, begin sewing the binding to the quilt with a ¼" seam.

For Mitered Corners:

1. Stop ¼" from the first corner. Leave the needle in the quilt and turn it 90°. Hit the reverse button on your machine and back off the quilt leaving the threads connected.

2. Fold the binding perpendicular to the side you sewed, making a 45° angle. Carefully maintaining the first fold, bring the binding back along the edge to be sewn.

3. Carefully align the edges of the binding with the quilt edge and sew as you did the first side. Repeat this process until you reach the tail left at the beginning. Fold the tail out of the way and sew until you are ¼" from the beginning stitches.

4. Remove the quilt from the machine. Fold the quilt out of the way and match the binding tails together. Carefully sew the binding tails with a ¼" seam. You can do this by hand if you prefer.

Finishing the Binding:

5. Trim the seam to reduce bulk.

6. Finish stitching the binding to the quilt across the join you just sewed.

7. Turn the binding to the back of the quilt. To reduce bulk at the corners, fold the miter in the opposite direction from which it was folded on the front.

8. Hand-sew a Blind stitch on the back of the quilt to secure the binding in place.

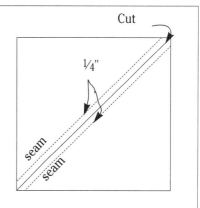

Half-Square Triangle
1. Place 2 squares right sides together.
2. Draw a diagonal line from corner to corner.
3. Stitch ¼" on each side of the line.
4. Cut squares apart on the diagonal line.
5. Open the 2 new squares with 2 colors.
6. Press. Trim off dog-ears.
7. Center and trim to size.

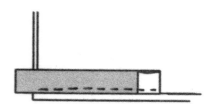

Align the raw edge of the binding with the raw edge of the quilt top. Start about 8" from the corner and go along the first side with a ¼" seam.

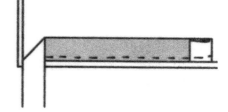

Stop ¼" from the edge. Then stitch a slant to the corner (through both layers of binding)... lift up, then down, as you line up the edge. Fold the binding back.

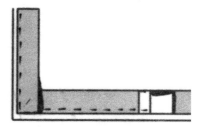

Align the raw edge again. Continue stitching the next side with a ¼" seam as you sew the binding in place.

Grand Old Flag

photos are on pages 48 - 49

SIZE: 49" x 64"

YARDAGE:
Colors - We used a *Moda* "Marbles Bright"
    'Jelly Roll' collection of $2\frac{1}{2}$" fabric strips
    - we purchased 1 'Jelly Roll'

5 strips	OR	$\frac{3}{8}$ yard Color B - Green
7 strips	OR	$\frac{1}{2}$ yard Color C - Red
4 strips	OR	$\frac{1}{3}$ yard Color D - Black
3 strips	OR	$\frac{1}{4}$ yard Color E - Light Blue
5 strips	OR	$\frac{3}{8}$ yard Color F - Dark Blue

White Fabric - We used a *Moda* "Basics" White
    'Jelly Roll' collection of $2\frac{1}{2}$" fabric strips
    - we purchased 1 'Jelly Roll'
    14 strips   OR   1 yard Color A - White

Border #5 & Binding   Purchase $1\frac{5}{8}$ yards
Backing   Purchase $2\frac{7}{8}$ yards
Batting   Purchase 57" x 72"
Sewing machine, needle, thread

Disappearing or Wash-out Marking Pen
Optional: Lightweight White iron-on interfacing - $8\frac{1}{2}$" for Star

PREPARATION FOR STRIPS:
    Cut all strips $2\frac{1}{2}$" by the width of fabric (usually 42" - 44").

CUTTING:
    Refer to the Cutting Chart.
    Label the pieces as you cut.

CUTTING CHART

Quantity	Length	Position
Color A - White		
6	25"	Stripes in Columns #2, #3, #4
3	10"	Stripes in Column #1
4	$8\frac{1}{2}$"	Star Applique
Color C - Red		
3	26"	Star Appliques
7	25"	Stripes in Columns #2, #3, #4
3	10"	Stripes in Column #1
Color B - Green		
1	25"	Columns #2, #3, #4
2	10"	Stripes in Column #1
Color F - Dark Blue		
3	39"	Star Appliques
3	20"	Background for Star

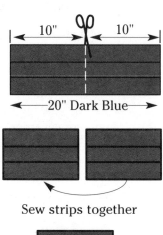

20" Dark Blue

Sew strips together

10" x $12\frac{1}{2}$" Dark Blue

MAKE THE FLAG:
Refer to the Section diagrams.

Column #1:

Background for the Large White Star :
    Sew 3 Dark Blue $2\frac{1}{2}$" x 20" strips together to
        make a piece $6\frac{1}{2}$" x 20". Press.
    Cut the strip into 2 pieces $6\frac{1}{2}$" x 10".
    Sew the pieces together to make a piece 10" x $12\frac{1}{2}$". Press.

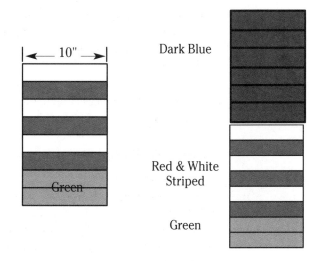

Stripes and Assembly:
    Sew 6 strips together alternating colors:
        3 of White $2\frac{1}{2}$" x 10" and
        3 of Red $2\frac{1}{2}$" x 10" to make a piece 10" x $12\frac{1}{2}$". Press.

    Sew 2 Green $2\frac{1}{2}$" x 10" strips to the bottom to make a
        piece 10" x $16\frac{1}{2}$" to complete Column #1. Press.

    Sew the White and Red striped section to the bottom
        of the Dark Blue to make a piece 10" x $28\frac{1}{2}$". Press.

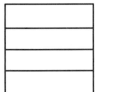

Sew 4 White Strips together to cut out Star Applique.

Prepare White Fabric for the Large White Star:
Set your sewing machine for a shorter than usual stitch length.
Sew 4 White $8\frac{1}{2}$" strips together to make a piece $8\frac{1}{2}$" x $8\frac{1}{2}$".
Press the seams open.

Cut Out the Large White Star:
Optional: Cut a star out from lightweight iron-on White interfacing. Center and press the interfacing on the wrong side of the White star section so that it will keep dark from 'shadowing' through the star.

Cut out the star applique using the pattern on pages 34 - 35. (Add $\frac{1}{4}$" seam allowance if you are turning the edges under).

Applique the Large White Star:
Refer to applique instructions.
Applique the large White star to the Blue background as desired.

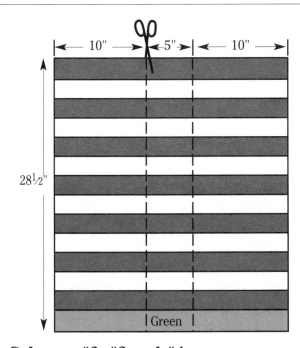

Columns #2, #3 and #4:

Sew the Striped Strip-Sets:

Sew 7 Red and 6 White 25" strips together alternating the colors beginning and ending with Red, to make a piece 25" x $26\frac{1}{2}$". Press.

Sew 1 Green 25" strip to the bottom of the piece. Press.

Cut the strip-set into 3 sections:
Cut Column #2 to 10" x $28\frac{1}{2}$". Press.
Cut Column #3 to 5" x $28\frac{1}{2}$". Press.
Cut Column #4 to 10" x $28\frac{1}{2}$". Press.

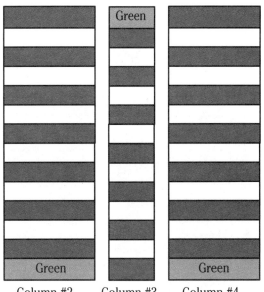

Column #2   Column #3   Column #4

Assemble the Columns into a Flag:

Arrange Columns #2 & #4 with Red on top.
Arrange Column #3 with Green on top.
Sew Columns #1, #2, #3 and #4 together. Press.

Embroider Words on the Flag:

Words - Trace or draw words with a Wash-out or Disappearing marking pen.
Embroider the words with Long Straight Stitches.

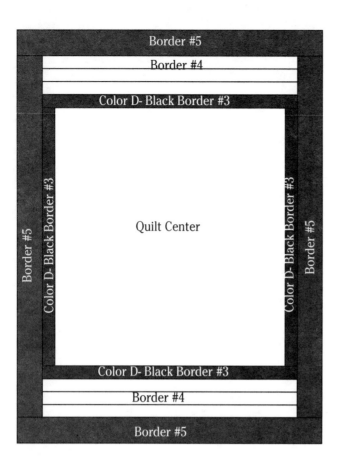

Border #4 - Top and Bottom Borders - White:
Cut 6 White strips $41\frac{1}{2}$" long.
Sew 3 White $41\frac{1}{2}$" strips together to make a piece
$6\frac{1}{2}$" x $41\frac{1}{2}$". Press. Make 2.
Sew a strip to the top and bottom of the quilt. Press.

Border #5 - Outer Border - Black:
Cut strips $4\frac{1}{2}$" wide parallel to the selvage
to eliminate piecing.
Cut 2 strips $4\frac{1}{2}$" x $56\frac{1}{2}$" for sides.
Cut 2 strips $4\frac{1}{2}$" x $49\frac{1}{2}$" for top and bottom.
Sew side borders to the quilt. Press.
Sew top and bottom borders to the quilt. Press.

BORDERS:
Border #1 - Color B - Green:
Cut 2 strips $2\frac{1}{2}$" x $28\frac{1}{2}$" for the sides.
Cut 2 strips $2\frac{1}{2}$" x $37\frac{1}{2}$" for top and bottom.
Sew side borders to the quilt. Press.
Sew top and bottom borders to the quilt. Press.

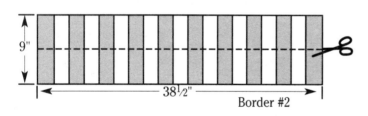

Border #2 - Light Blue and White:
Cut 9 White $2\frac{1}{2}$" x 9" strips.
Cut 10 Light Blue $2\frac{1}{2}$" x 9" strips.
Sew the Piano Key Strip-Sets:
Sew 10 Light Blue and 9 White $2\frac{1}{2}$" x 9" strips together
alternating the colors, beginning and ending with
Light Blue to make a piece 9" x $38\frac{1}{2}$". Press.
Cut the strip-set into 2 sections, each $4\frac{1}{2}$" x $38\frac{1}{2}$".
Add to the Top and Bottom of Quilt:
Center and sew 1 section to the top and 1 section to
the bottom of the quilt. Press. Trim off any excess.

Border #3 - Color D - Black:
Cut 2 strips $2\frac{1}{2}$" x $40\frac{1}{2}$" for sides.
Cut 2 strips $2\frac{1}{2}$" x $41\frac{1}{2}$" for top and bottom.
Sew side borders to the quilt. Press.
Sew top and bottom borders to the quilt. Press.

Grand Old Flag
Small Star Pattern
Cut 6 Blue
Cut 4 Red

Add a scant $\frac{1}{4}$" seam
allowance around pieces
before cutting.

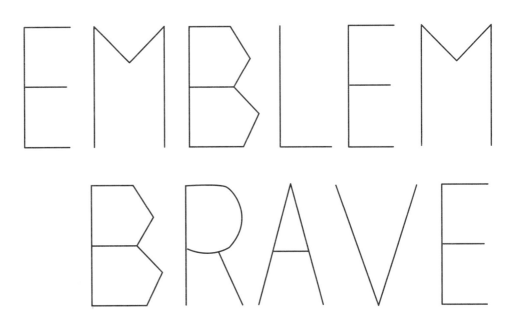

APPLIQUE STARS:

Small Applique Stars:

Sew 3 Dark Blue 39" strips together side by side.
Sew 3 Red 26" strips together side by side.
Press the seams open

Cut Out the Small Stars:

Cut out the star appliques using the pattern
on page 32.
Cut 6 Dark Blue stars.
Cut 4 Red stars.
(Add $1/4$" seam allowance if you are turning the
edges under).

Applique the Small Stars:

Refer to applique instructions.
Applique the stars to the White background
(Border #4) as desired.

FINISHING:

Quilting:

See Basic Instructions.

Binding:

Cut strips $2^1/2$" wide.
Sew together end to end to equal 236".
See Binding Instructions.

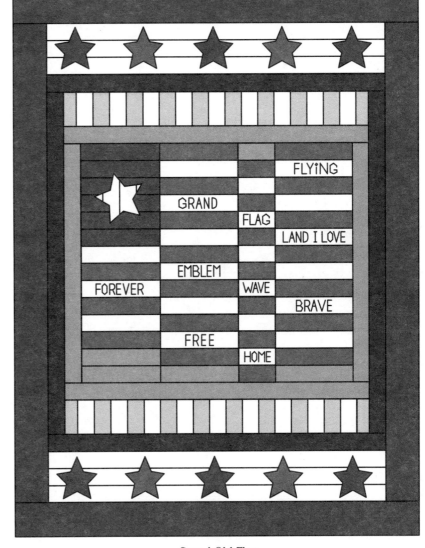

Grand Old Flag
Finished Assembly Diagram

GRAND
FLYING
FLAG
LAND I LOVE
FOREVER

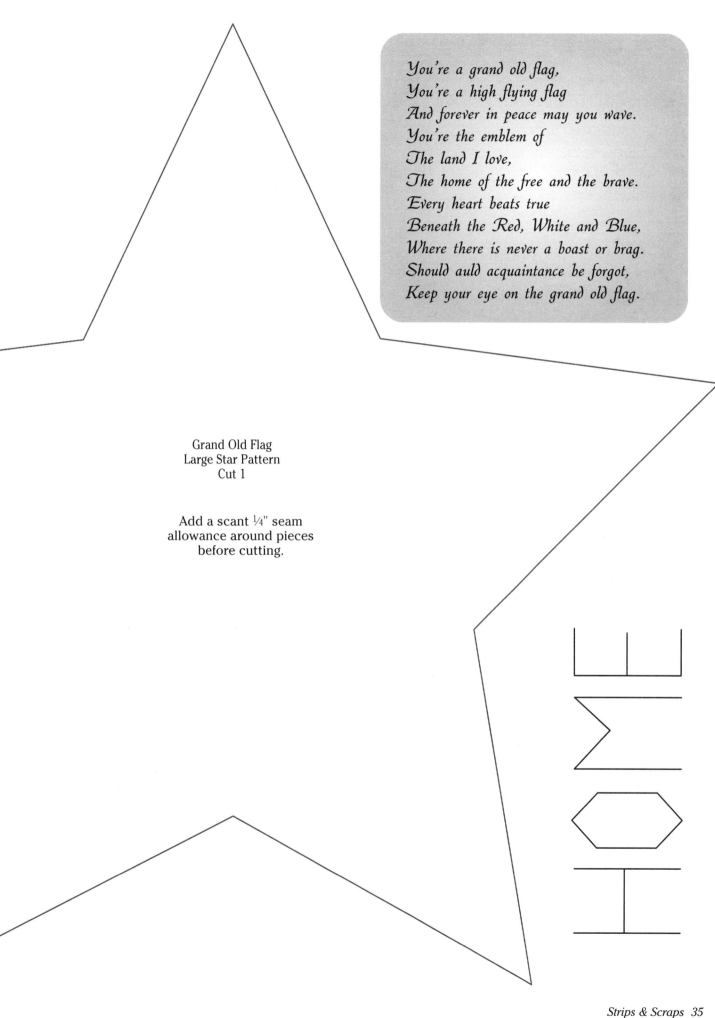

You're a grand old flag,
You're a high flying flag
And forever in peace may you wave.
You're the emblem of
The land I love,
The home of the free and the brave.
Every heart beats true
Beneath the Red, White and Blue,
Where there is never a boast or brag.
Should auld acquaintance be forgot,
Keep your eye on the grand old flag.

Grand Old Flag
Large Star Pattern
Cut 1

Add a scant ¼" seam
allowance around pieces
before cutting.

HOME

Something for Everyone

photos are on pages 46, 50 - 51

SIZE: 66" x 78"

YARDAGE:
We used a *Moda* "The Caroler" by Mary Engelbreit
    'Jelly Roll' collection of $2\frac{1}{2}$" fabric strips
    - we purchased 1 'Jelly Roll'
    4 strips   OR $\frac{1}{3}$ yard Color B - Blue
    4 strips   OR $\frac{1}{3}$ yard Color C - Red
    7 strips   OR $\frac{1}{2}$ yard Color D - White
    5 strips   OR $\frac{3}{8}$ yard Color E - Yellow
    4 strips   OR $\frac{1}{3}$ yard Color G - Green
We used a *Moda* "Basics" Black
    'Jelly Roll' collection of $2\frac{1}{2}$" fabric strips
    - we purchased 1 'Jelly Roll'
    35 strips   OR $2\frac{1}{2}$ yards Color A - Black
Border #3 & Binding   Purchase 2 yards Black print
Backing   Purchase $5\frac{1}{8}$ yards
Batting   Purchase 74" x 86"
Sewing machine, needle, thread
DMC pearl cotton or 6-ply floss
#22 or #24 chenille needle

PREPARATION FOR STRIPS:
    Cut all strips $2\frac{1}{2}$" by the width of fabric (usually 42" - 44").
    Label the stacks or pieces as you cut.

SEW BLOCKS:
    Refer to the
        Cutting Chart and
        Assembly instructions
        for each block.
    Label the pieces
        as you cut.

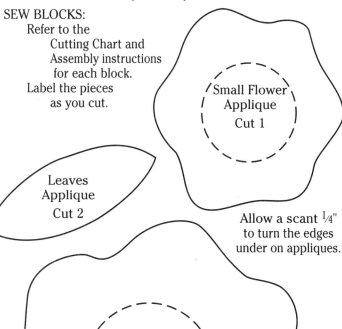

Small Flower
Applique
Cut 1

Leaves
Applique
Cut 2

Large Flower
Applique
Cut 1

Allow a scant $\frac{1}{4}$"
to turn the edges
under on appliques.

Center
Applique
Cut 2

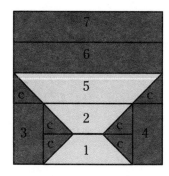

Snowball Corners

Align a square with each corner. Draw a diagonal lin as shown and sew on the line. Fold the corner back and press. Repeat for all corners.

Flower Vase · Block 1

CUTTING CHART

Quantity	Length	Position
Color E - Yellow		
1	$10\frac{1}{2}$"	#5
2	$6\frac{1}{2}$"	#1, 2
Color G - Green		
1	9"	Applique
Color C - Red		
1	$10\frac{1}{2}$"	Applique
Color A - Black		
2	$10\frac{1}{2}$"	#6, 7
2	$4\frac{1}{2}$"	#3, 4
6	$2\frac{1}{2}$"	#1c, 1c, 2c, 2c, 5c, 5c

ASSEMBLY:
Refer to Snowball Corner instructions.
    Align 1 Snowball square on each end of #1, 2, & 5.
    Sew on the diagonal, fold back pieces. Press.
Refer to the Block 1 diagram.
    Sew #1-2. Press.
    Sew #3 & #4 to the left and right sides of the piece. Press.
    Sew #5, #6, & #7 to the top of the piece. Press.
Refer to the Applique instructions.
    Cut 2 Red $3\frac{1}{2}$" strips and sew them together to make
        the large flower.
    Cut out pieces using patterns. Applique as desired.
    Embroider stems with long and short Running stitches.

Completed Applique Block

House · Block 2

CUTTING CHART

Quantity	Length	Position
Color B - Blue		
1	10½"	#8
1	6½"	#9
Color C - Red		
1	10½"	#7
3	4½"	#3, 4, 6
1	2½"	#1
Color E - Yellow		
1	4½"	#5
1	2½"	#2
Color A - Black		
6	2½"	#8c, 8c, 9c, 9c, 10, 11

ASSEMBLY:
Refer to Snowball Corner instructions.
  Align 1 Snowball square on each end of #8 & 9.
  For each Snowball square, sew on the diagonal, fold back the top layer and press.
Sew #10 & 11 to the left and right sides of #9. Press.
Sew #1-2. Press.
Sew #3 to the left side of #1-2. Press.
Sew #4, 5, & 6 to the right side of the piece. Press.
Sew #7, 8, & 9 to the top of the piece. Press.

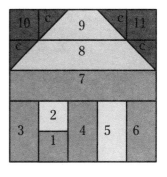

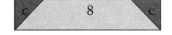

Tall Pine · Block 3

CUTTING CHART

Quantity	Length	Position
Color G - Green		
3	6½"	#1, 2, 3
1	4½"	#10
Color E - Yellow		
1	2½"	#7
Color A - Black		
2	6½"	#4, 5
2	4½"	#6, 8
2	3½"	#9, 11
8	2½"	#1c, 1,c, 2c, 2c, #3c, 3,c, 10c, 10c

ASSEMBLY:
Refer to Snowball Corner instructions.
  Align a Snowball square on each end of #1,2, 3 & 10.
  For each Snowball square, sew on the diagonal, fold back the top layer and press.
Sew #1-2-3 together. Press.
Sew #4 & 5 to the left and right sides of the piece. Press.
Sew #6-7-8 together. Press.
  Sew to the bottom of the piece. Press.
Sew #9-10-11 together. Press.
  Sew to the top of the piece. Press.

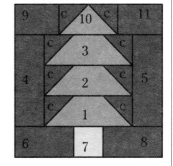

Little Bird · Block 4

CUTTING CHART

Quantity	Length	Position
Color B - Blue		
1	6½"	#5
1	4½"	#3
1	2½"	#2
Color A - Black		
2	10½"	#8, 9
2	6½"	#6, 7
1	4½"	#4
2	2½"	#1, 5c

ASSEMBLY:
Refer to Snowball Corner instructions.
  Align 1 Snowball square on the end of #5.
  Sew on the diagonal, fold back the top layer and press.
Sew #1-2. Press.
Sew #3 to the right side of #1-2. Press.
Sew #4 to the top of the piece. Press.
Sew #5 to the left side of #1-2. Press.
Sew #6 & 7 to the top and bottom of the piece. Press.
Sew #8 & 9 to the left and right sides of the piece. Press.
Embroider the beak, eye, and legs with long and short Running stitches.

Embroidery Eye and Beak Patterns

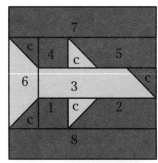

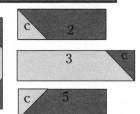

Shark · Block 5

CUTTING CHART

Quantity	Length	Position
Color B - Blue		
1	$8\frac{1}{2}$"	#3
1	$6\frac{1}{2}$"	#6
2	$2\frac{1}{2}$"	#2c, 5c
Color A - Black		
2	$10\frac{1}{2}$"	#7, 8
2	$6\frac{1}{2}$"	#2, 5
5	$2\frac{1}{2}$"	#1, 3c, 4, 6c, 6c

ASSEMBLY:
Refer to Snowball Corner instructions.

Align 1 Snowball square on the end of #2, #3 and #5.

Align a Snowball square on each end of #6.

Sew on the diagonal, fold back the top layer and press.

Sew #1-2. Press.

Sew #4-5. Press.

Sew #1-2 and #4-5 to the bottom and top of #3. Press.

Sew #6 to the left side of the piece. Press.

Sew #7 & 8 to the top and bottom of the piece. Press.

Embroider the eye with tiny Running stitches.

Flower · Block 6

CUTTING CHART

Quantity	Length	Position
Color E - Yellow		
2	$6\frac{1}{2}$"	#4, 5
2	$2\frac{1}{2}$"	#1, 3
Color C - Red		
1	$2\frac{1}{2}$"	#2
Color G - Green		
1	$4\frac{1}{2}$"	#7
1	5"	Applique
Color A - Black		
2	$10\frac{1}{2}$"	#9, 10
2	$4\frac{1}{2}$"	#6, 8
4	$2\frac{1}{2}$"	#4c, 4c, 5c, 5c

ASSEMBLY:
Refer to Snowball Corner instructions.

Align 1 Snowball square on each end of #4 & #5.

For each Snowball square, sew on the diagonal, fold back the top layer and press.

Flower: Sew #1-2-3. Press.

Sew #4 & 5 to the left and right sides of the piece. Press.

Stem: Sew #6-7-8. Press.

Finish: Sew the Flower to the Stem section. Press.

Sew #9 & 10 to the left and right sides of the piece. Press.

Refer to the Applique instructions.

Cut out 2 leaves and applique as desired.

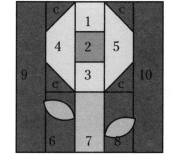

Leaves
Applique - Make 2

Allow a scant $\frac{1}{4}$" to turn the edges under on appliques.

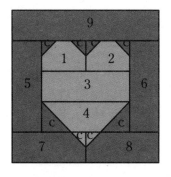

Heart · Block 7

CUTTING CHART

Quantity	Length	Position
Color C - Red		
2	$6\frac{1}{2}$"	#3, 4
2	$3\frac{1}{2}$"	#1, 2
2	$1\frac{1}{2}$" x $1\frac{1}{2}$"	#7c, 8c
Color A - Black		
1	$10\frac{1}{2}$"	#9
2	$6\frac{1}{2}$"	#5, 6
2	$5\frac{1}{2}$"	#7, 8
2	$2\frac{1}{2}$"	#4c, 4c
4	$1\frac{1}{2}$" x $1\frac{1}{2}$"	#1c, 1c, 2c, 2c

ASSEMBLY:
Refer to Snowball Corner instructions.

Align a $1\frac{1}{2}$" Color A Snowball square on each end of #1 & 2.

Align a $2\frac{1}{2}$" Color A Snowball square on each end of #4.

Align a $1\frac{1}{2}$" Color C Snowball square on 1 end of #7 & 8.

For each Snowball square, sew on the diagonal, fold back the top layer and press.

Sew #1-2. Press.

Sew #3 & #4 to the bottom of the piece. Press.

Sew #5 & #6 to the left and right sides of the piece. Press.

Sew #7-8. Press.

Sew #7-8 to the bottom and #9 to the top of the piece. Press.

Maple Leaf · Block 8

CUTTING CHART

Quantity	Length	Position
Color G - Green		
7	2½"	#2, 3, 4, 5, 6, 7, 8
1	2" x 3½"	stem applique on #9
Color A - Black		
2	10½"	#12, 13
2	6½"	#10, 11
6	2½"	#1, 2c, 3c, 4c, 7c, 9

ASSEMBLY:

Applique for Stem - Square #9:

Fold the stem in half lengthwise to make a piece 1" x 3½".

Sew a ¼" seam along the long edge and turn right side out.

Press with the seam centered on the back.

Applique the stem to square #9. Press.

Tip: Do not sew half-square triangles for #2, 3, 4 & 7 or the finished squares will be too small.

Refer to Snowball Corner instructions.

Align a 2½" Snowball square on #2, 3, 4 & 7.

For each Snowball square, sew on the diagonal, fold back the top layer and press.

Refer to the Block 8 diagram.

Row 1: Sew #1-2-3. Press.

Row 2: Sew #4-5-6. Press.

Row 3: Sew #7-8-9. Press.

Sew the rows together. Press.

Borders: Sew #10 & 11 to the left and right sides of the piece. Press.

Sew #12 & 13 to the top and bottom of the piece. Press.

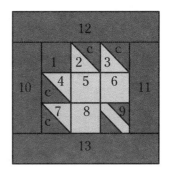

 Stem Applique

Scotty Dog · Block 9

CUTTING CHART

Quantity	Length	Position
Color D - White		
2	8½"	#4, 5
1	4½"	#8
4	2½"	#1, 3, 7c, 9c
Color A - Black		
3	6½"	#6, 7, 10
2	4½"	#2, 9

Embroidery Eye, Nose and Mouth Patterns

ASSEMBLY:

Refer to Snowball Corner instructions.

Align a 2½" Snowball square on #7 & 9.

For each Snowball square, sew on the diagonal, fold back the top layer and press.

Refer to the Block 3 diagram.

Sew #1-2-3. Press.

Sew #4 & 5 to the top of the piece. Press.

Sew #6 to the right side of the piece. Press.

Sew #7-8. Press.

Sew #9-10. Press.

Sew #7-8 and #9-10 to the top of the piece. Press.

Embroider nose, eye and mouth.

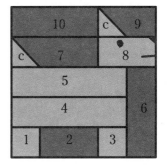

Bird · Block 10

CUTTING CHART

Quantity	Length	Position
Color C - Red		
2	6½"	#1, 2
2	2½"	#3c, 7
3	2" x 2"	#3c, 4c, 5c
Color A - Black		
2	10½"	#8, 9
1	6½"	#3
2	4½"	#4, 6
3	2½"	#1c, 1c, 5

Embroidery Beak and Eye Patterns

ASSEMBLY:

Refer to Snowball Corner instructions.

Align a 2½" Snowball square on each end of #1 and the right end of #3.

Align a 2" Snowball square on #4 & 5 and on the left end of #3.

For each Snowball corner, sew on the diagonal, fold back the top layer and press.

Refer to the Block 10 diagram.

Sew #1-2-3. Press.

Sew #4-5. Press.

Sew #6-7. Press.

Sew #4-5 and #6-7 to the left and right sides of the piece. Press.

Sew #8 and #9 to the top and bottom of the piece. Press.

Embroider beak and eye.

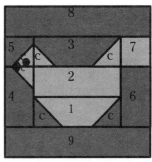

Bird Block 10

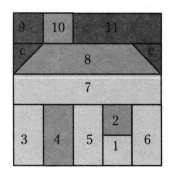

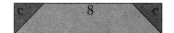

House · Block 11

CUTTING CHART

Quantity	Length	Position
Color C - Red		
1	10½"	#8
1	4½"	#4
2	2½"	#2, 10
Color B - Blue		
1	10½"	#7
3	4½"	#3, 5, 6
1	2½"	#1
Color A - Black		
1	6½"	#11
3	2½"	#8c, 8c, 9

ASSEMBLY:
Refer to Snowball Corner instructions.
　　Align a Snowball square on each end of #8.
　　For each Snowball corner, sew on the diagonal, fold back the top layer and press.
Refer to the Block 11 diagram.
　　Sew #1-2. Press.
　　Sew #3, 4 & 5 to the left side of the piece. Press.
　　Sew #6 to the right side of the piece. Press.
　　Sew #7 & 8 to the top of the piece. Press.
　　Sew #9-10-11. Press.
　　Sew #9-10-11 to the top of the piece. Press.

Flower Basket · Block 12

CUTTING CHART

Quantity	Length	Position
Color E - Yellow		
2	10½"	#1, 2
Color A - Black		
3	10½"	#3, 4, 5
4	2½"	#1c, 1c, 2c, 2c
Color C - Red		
1	8"	Applique
Color G - Green		
1	10"	Applique

FLOWER BASKET BLOCK 12 ASSEMBLY:
Snowball Corners:
Refer to Snowball Corner instructions.
　　Align a Snowball square on each end of #1 & 2.
　　For each Snowball corner, sew on the diagonal, fold back the top layer and press.
Refer to the Block 12 diagram.
Sew #1-2-3-4-5. Press.
Applique flowers and leaves at this time if desired.
Refer to the Applique instructions.
Embroider stems with long and short Running Stitches.

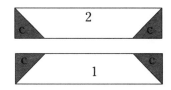

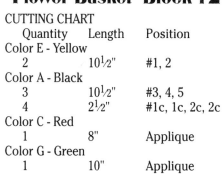

Applique Placement

Leaf
Applique
Cut 3

Allow a scant ¼" to
turn the edges under on
appliques.

Flower
Applique
Cut 3

Allow a scant ¼" to
turn the edges under on
appliques.

Tree · Block 13

CUTTING CHART

Quantity	Length	Position
Color G - Green		
3	6½"	#1, 2, 3
Color E - Yellow		
1	4½"	#5
Color A - Black		
2	10½"	#7, 8
2	4½"	#4, 6
4	2½"	#1c, 1c, 3c, 3c

ASSEMBLY:
Snowball Corners:
Refer to the Snowball Corner instructions.
Align a 2½" Snowball Corner square on each end of #1 & #3.
For each Snowball square, sew on the diagonal, fold back the top layer and press.

Refer to the Block 13 diagram.
Top: Sew #1-2-3. Press.
Bottom: Sew #4-5-6. Press.
Sew the Top and Bottom pieces together. Press.
Sew #7 & #8 to the left and right sides of the piece. Press.

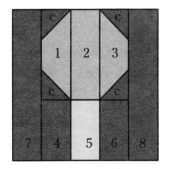

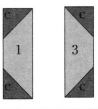

Short Pine · Block 14

CUTTING CHART

Quantity	Length	Position
Color G - Green		
1	8½"	#5
1	6½"	#8
1	4½"	#11
Color E - Yellow		
1	2½"	#2
Color A - Black		
1	10½"	#13
2	4½"	#1, 3
2	3½"	#10, 12
8	2½"	#5c, 5c, 7, 8c, 8c, 9, 11c, 11c
2	1½"	#4, 6

ASSEMBLY:
Snowball Corners:
Refer to the Snowball Corner instructions.
Align a 2½" Snowball Corner square on each end of #5, 8 & #11.
For each Snowball square, sew on the diagonal, fold back the top layer and press.

Refer to the Block 14 diagram.
Row 1: Sew #1-2-3. Press.
Row 2: Sew #4-5-6. Press.
Row 3: Sew #7-8-9. Press.
Row 4: Sew #10-11-12. Press.
Sew the rows together. Press.
Sew #13 to the top of the piece. Press.

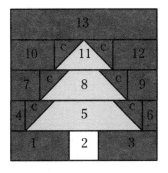

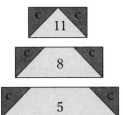

Cat · Block 15

CUTTING CHART

Quantity	Length	Position
Color E - Yellow		
1	10½"	#7
1	6½"	#4
2	4½"	#8, 12
4	2½"	#1, 3, 10c, 10c
1	1½" x 1½"	#9c
Color A - Black		
5	4½"	#5, 6, 9, 10, 11
3	2½"	#2, 7c, 7c

Cat Face Embroidery Patterns

ASSEMBLY:
Snowball Corners:
Refer to the Snowball Corner instructions.
Align a 2½" Snowball Corner square on each end of #7 & #10.
Align a 1½" Snowball Corner square on 1 end of #9 as shown.
For each Snowball square, sew on the diagonal, fold back the top layer, press.

Bottom Section:
Sew #1-2-3. Press.
Sew #4 to the top of the piece. Press.
Sew #5 & #6 to the left and right sides of piece.
Sew #7 to the top of the piece. Press.

Top Section:
Sew #8-9. Press.
Sew #10-11. Press.
Sew #8-9 to #10-11. Press.
Sew #12 to the right side of the piece. Press.
Sew the top and bottom sections together. Press.

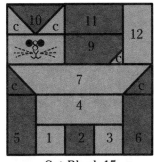

Cat Block 15

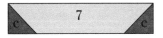

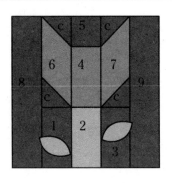

Tulip · Block 16

CUTTING CHART

Quantity	Length	Position
Color C - Red		
2	$6\frac{1}{2}$"	#6, 7
1	$4\frac{1}{2}$"	#4
Color G - Green		
1	$4\frac{1}{2}$"	#2
1	5"	Applique
Color A - Black		
2	$10\frac{1}{2}$"	#8, 9
2	$4\frac{1}{2}$"	#1, 3
5	$2\frac{1}{2}$"	#5, 6c, 6c, 7c, 7c

Leaves
Cut 2
Green

Allow a acant $\frac{1}{4}$" to turn the edges under.

ASSEMBLY:

Snowball Corners:
Refer to the Snowball Corner instructions.
Align 1 Snowball Corner square on each end of #6 & #7.
For each Snowball square, sew on the diagonal, fold back the top layer and press.

Stem Section:
Sew #1-2-3. Press.

Flower Section:
Sew $4-5. Press.
Sew #6 & 7 to the left and right sides of #4-5. Press.
Sew the sections together. Press.
Sew #8 & #9 to the left and right sides of the piece. Press.

Applique Leaves:
Cut out 2 Green leaves using patterns.
Applique as desired.

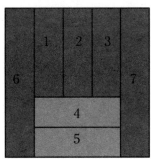

Embroidery Flower Center

Applique Placement

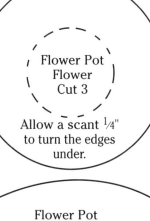

Flower Pot
Flower
Cut 3

Allow a scant $\frac{1}{4}$" to turn the edges under.

Flower Pot
Leaves
Cut 3

Allow a scant $\frac{1}{4}$" to turn the edges under.

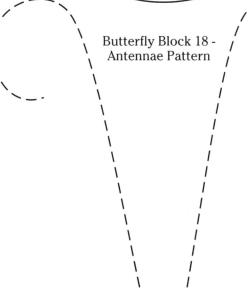

Butterfly Block 18 - Antennae Pattern

Flower Pot · Block 17

CUTTING CHART

Quantity	Length	Position
Color C - Red		
2	$6\frac{1}{2}$"	#4, 5
Color A - Black		
2	$10\frac{1}{2}$"	#6, 7
3	$6\frac{1}{2}$"	#1, 2, 3
Color G - Green		
1	$10\frac{1}{2}$"	Applique
Color E - Yellow		
1	$7\frac{1}{2}$"	Applique

ASSEMBLY:

Sew #1-2-3. Press.
Sew #4 & 5 to the bottom of the piece. Press
Sew #6 & 7 to the left and right sides of the piece. Press.

Refer to the Applique instructions.
Cut out pieces and applique as desired.
Embroider stems with Running Stitches.

Butterfly · Block 18

CUTTING CHART

Quantity	Length	Position
Color E - Yellow		
2	10½"	#3, 6
2	8½"	#2, 7
2	2½"	#1, 8
Color G - Green		
1	8½"	#4
Color A - Black		
7	2½"	#1c, 2c, 3c, 5, 6c, 7c, 8c

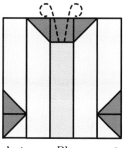

Antenna Placement

ASSEMBLY:
Refer to Snowball Corner instructions.
Align 1 Snowball square on #1, 2, 3, 6, 7, & 8.
TIP: Aligning a Snowball square on
#1 and #8 may seem a little tricky.
Simply align the squares and note
the direction of the diagonal.
(Do not sew two 2½"x 2½" squares
to make half square triangles or
they will turn out too small.)
Sew on the diagonal, fold back pieces. Press.
Sew #1-2, #4-5, and #7-8. Press.

Sew the columns together. Press.

Embroidery:
Since the antennae extend into the sashing,
the embroidery is done after the quilt is
assembled. Use long Running Stitches.

Running Stitch

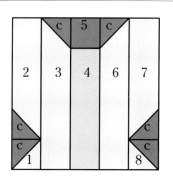

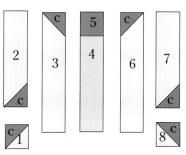

Fish · Block 19

CUTTING CHART

Quantity	Length	Position
Color B - Blue		
2	8½"	#1, 2
1	4½"	#3
1	2½"	#4c
Color A - Black		
2	10½"	#6, 7
1	6½"	#4
1	4½"	#5
6	2½"	#1c, 1c, 2c, 2c, 3c, 3c

Embroidery Fish Eye
Pattern

ASSEMBLY:
Snowball Corners:
Refer to the Snowball Corner instructions.
Align 1 Color A Snowball Corner square on
each end of #1, #2, & #3.
Align 1 Color B Snowball Corner square on #4.
For each Snowball square, sew on the diagonal,
fold back the top layer and press.

Assembly:
Sew #1-2. Press.
Sew #3 to the right side of the piece. Press.
Sew #4-5. Press.
Sew #4-5 to the top of the piece. Press.
Sew #6 & #7 to the top and bottom of the piece.
Press.
Embroider eye on fish.

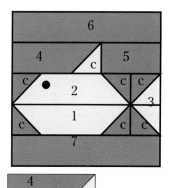

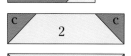

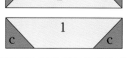

Home · Block 20

CUTTING CHART

Quantity	Length	Position
Color B - Blue		
1	10½"	#8
1	6½"	#9
Color E - Yellow		
1	4½"	#5
1	2½"	#2
Color C - Red		
1	10½"	#7
3	4½"	#3, 4, 6
1	2½"	#1
Color A - Black		
6	2½"	#8c, 8c, 9c, 9c, 10, 11

ASSEMBLY:
Snowball Corners:
Refer to the Snowball Corner instructions.
Align 1 Color B Snowball Corner square on each
end of #8 & #9.
For each Snowball square, sew on the diagonal,
fold back the top layer and press.

Refer to the Block 20 diagram.
Sew #10 & #11 to the left and right sides of #9.
Press.
Sew #1-2. Press.
Sew #3 on the right side of #1-2. Press.
Sew #4, 5 & 6 to the left side of the piece. Press.
Sew #7, 8, & 9 to the top of the piece. Press.

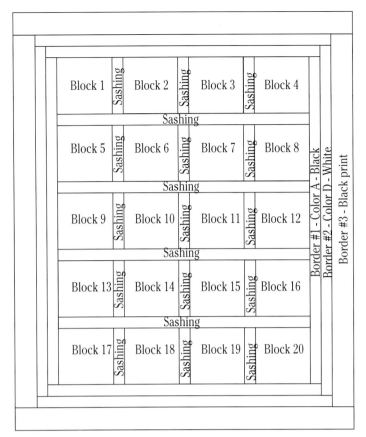

The diagram shows a grid of blocks with sashing:

Block 1 — Sashing — Block 2 — Sashing — Block 3 — Sashing — Block 4
Sashing
Block 5 — Sashing — Block 6 — Sashing — Block 7 — Sashing — Block 8
Sashing
Block 9 — Sashing — Block 10 — Sashing — Block 11 — Sashing — Block 12
Sashing
Block 13 — Sashing — Block 14 — Sashing — Block 15 — Sashing — Block 16
Sashing
Block 17 — Sashing — Block 18 — Sashing — Block 19 — Sashing — Block 20

Border #1 - Color A - Black
Border #2 - Color D - White
Border #3 - Black print

Something for Everyone - Assembly Diagram

SASHINGS:
From Color A - Black:
Cut 15 Vertical Sashes $2\frac{1}{2}$" x $10\frac{1}{2}$".
Cut 4 Horizontal Sashes $2\frac{1}{2}$" x $46\frac{1}{2}$".

ASSEMBLY:
Refer to the Quilt Assembly diagram.
Arrange all blocks and sashing strips on a
    work surface or table.

For Each Row:
Use $10\frac{1}{2}$" vertical sashing strips between the blocks.
Sew Block - Sash - Block - Sash - Block - Sash - Block.
    Press. Make 5 rows.

Sew Rows and Sashing Together:
Use $46\frac{1}{2}$" horizontal sashing strips between the rows.
Sew the rows together with a Sashing strip between
    each row. Press.

BORDERS:
Border #1:
From Color A - Black:
Cut strips $2\frac{1}{2}$" by the width of fabric.
Sew strips together end to end.

Cut 2 strips $2\frac{1}{2}$" x $58\frac{1}{2}$" for sides.
Cut 2 strips $2\frac{1}{2}$" x $50\frac{1}{2}$" for top and bottom.
Sew side borders to the quilt. Press.
Sew top and bottom borders to the quilt. Press.

Border #2:
From Fabric D - White:
Cut strips $2\frac{1}{2}$" by the width of fabric.
Sew strips together end to end.

Cut 2 strips $2\frac{1}{2}$" x $62\frac{1}{2}$" for sides.
Cut 2 strips $2\frac{1}{2}$" x $54\frac{1}{2}$" for top and bottom.
Sew side borders to the quilt. Press.
Sew top and bottom borders to the quilt. Press.

Border #3:
From Black print:
Cut strips $6\frac{1}{2}$" wide parallel to the selvage to
    eliminate piecing.

Cut 2 strips $6\frac{1}{2}$" x $66\frac{1}{2}$" for sides.
Cut 2 strips $6\frac{1}{2}$" x $66\frac{1}{2}$" for top and bottom.
Sew side borders to the quilt. Press.
Sew top and bottom borders to the quilt. Press.

FINISHING:
Embroidery:
Embroider butterfly antennae with long and
    short Running stitches.
Quilting:
See Basic Instructions.
Binding:
Cut strips $2\frac{1}{2}$" wide.
Sew together end to end to equal 298".
See Binding Instructions.

Something for Everyone - Finished Diagram

Baby Quilt

Photo is on page 47

SIZE: 34" x 46"

YARDAGE:
We used a *Moda* "The Caroler" by Mary Engelbreit
 'Jelly Roll' collection of $2\frac{1}{2}$" fabric strips
   - we purchased 1 'Jelly Roll'
   6 strips   OR $\frac{1}{2}$ yard Color A - Ivory print
   2 strips   OR $\frac{1}{6}$ yard Color B - Blue print
   2 strips   OR $\frac{1}{6}$ yard Color C - Red print
   2 strips   OR $\frac{1}{6}$ yard Color E - Yellow print
   2 strips   OR $\frac{1}{6}$ yard Color G - Green print
Sashing   Purchase $\frac{3}{8}$ yards Black
Border & Binding   Purchase $1\frac{1}{8}$ yards Ivory print
Backing   Purchase $1\frac{1}{2}$ yards
Batting   Purchase 42" x 54"

Sewing machine, needle, thread
DMC pearl cotton or 6-ply floss
#22 or #24 chenille needle

PREPARATION FOR STRIPS:
   Cut all strips $2\frac{1}{2}$" by the width of fabric (usually 42" - 44").
   Label the stacks or pieces as you cut.

SEW BLOCKS:
   Refer to the Something for Everyone instructions
      on pages 36 - 38.
   Cut and sew each block substituting Ivory strips for
      the Color A - Black strips in each block.
   Block A - Little Bird - Block #4 on page 37.
   Block B - Flower - Block #6 on page 38.
   Block C - Tall Pine - Block #3 on page 37.
   Block D - House - Block #2 on page 37.
   Block E - Heart - Block #7 on page 38.
   Block F - Flower Vase - Block #1 on page 36.

SASHING STRIPS:
   Cut 17 strips $2\frac{1}{2}$" x $10\frac{1}{2}$".

CORNERSTONES:
   Cut 12 Blue squares $2\frac{1}{2}$" x $2\frac{1}{2}$".

ASSEMBLY:
Refer to the Quilt Assembly diagram.
Arrange all blocks and sashing strips on a table.
For Each Row:
   Sew Sash-Block-Sash-Block-Sash. Press.
   Make 3 rows.
Horizontal Sashing Strips:
   Sew Cornerstone-Sash-Cornerstone-
      Sash-Cornerstone. Press. Make 4.
   Sew the rows together with a sashing strip between
      each row. Press.
   Sew a sashing strip to the top and bottom of the piece.
      Press.

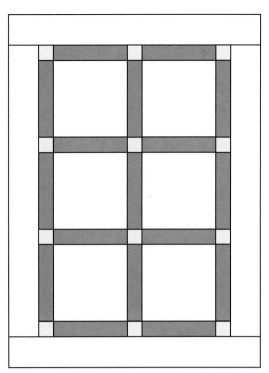

Baby Quilt - Assembly Diagram

Baby Quilt - Finished Diagram

BORDER:
Cut strips $4\frac{1}{2}$" wide parallel to the selvage to eliminate piecing.
   Cut 2 strips $4\frac{1}{2}$" x $38\frac{1}{2}$" for sides.
   Cut 2 strips $4\frac{1}{2}$" x $34\frac{1}{2}$" for top and bottom.

   Sew side borders to the quilt. Press.
   Sew top and bottom borders to the quilt. Press.

FINISHING:
Quilting: See Basic Instructions.
Binding: Cut strips $2\frac{1}{2}$" wide.
               Sew together end to end to equal 170".
               See Binding Instructions.

Mix and Match Blocks for Quilts

Flower Vase 1

House 2

Tall Pine 3

Little Bird 4

Shark 5

Flower 6

Heart 7

Maple Leaf 8

Scotty Dog 9

Bird 10

House 11

Flower Basket 12

Tree 13

Short Pine 14

Cat 15

Tulip 16

Flower Pot 17

Butterfly 18

Fish 19

Home 20

'The Caroler'
Jelly Roll

Baby Sampler

pieced by Rose Ann Pegram
quilted by Sue Needle

Break away from the traditional pastel baby quilt with something vivid and memorable.

Primary colors and clean lines make this quilt the perfect gift for a baby shower.

instructions on page 45

'Marbles Brights'
and a White'
Jelly Roll

Grand Old Flag

pieced by Donna Kinsey
quilted by Sue Needle

You're a grand old flag,
You're a high flying flag,
And forever in peace may you wave!
It's the home of the free because of the brave.
Celebrate your patriotism and capture the spirit of
this land we love with a high flying flag quilt.

instructions on pages 30 - 35